None of us enjoy livi a corrupt, dangerous society but so long as we sit back and take things easy, crime will continue to be a major problem.

This book looks at ways of detecting and preventing crime and avoiding illegal situations. It will enable you and your friends to fight crime and stay out of danger. This will reduce the fear of crime in your community making it a happier, more inviting place.

JOIN IN THE FIGHT AGAINST CRIME...

Published and copyright© by Kids Safetynet Limited.
This publication is protected by copyright. ISBN 1-903997-03-8

Thanks to Marian Fitton (Curriculum advice), Ellen Weaver and Godfrey Hall (Educational Consultants), Metropolitan Police Service, Central Scotland Police Service, South Yorkshire Police Service, West Yorkshire Police Service and Victim Support (Trafford) who helped with the project. Graphic Design - Jane Hart.

street
robbers
are
cowards
WE'RE GETTING A GRIP ON STREET ROBBERY
CALL:
CRIMESTOPPERS
ANONYMOUSLY ON
0800 555 111
help us
catch a
coward

Contents

Throughout the book there are a number of helpful ideas for your own crime prevention projects.

Youth Action Groups

Community Safety

Crime and the fear of crime are amongst the most serious problems facing society today, and young people are one of the most vulnerable groups.

Crime can be tackled and safer communities created, and an effective method of achieving this is by encouraging young people to deal with the problems themselves through Youth Action Groups.

A good example is the Lifestyle Project where young people took on summer holiday projects such as organising charity events and clearing up areas of their local environment.

Young people involved in the West Yorkshire Police Lifestyle Project

FOR MORE INFORMATION CONTACT:
THE SCHOOLS LIAISON OFFICER AT YOUR LOCAL POLICE STATION

Staying in control of your life

How many times have you agreed to do something that a friend wants to do just to avoid an argument. This may be a good way to keep a friend but could lead to big problems.

As we move through life from adolescence to adulthood, we find ourselves faced with more and more decisions. Constraints are put upon us by Law, but we can all exercise free choice. We can all make our own decisions and take responsibility for ourselves. Each and every one of us has a right to feel safe. With that right comes a responsibility to make sure that those around us feel safe with us.

If someone told us to jump from an aeroplane without a parachute, we'd tell them where to go in no uncertain terms!

We would know that what they are telling us to do is dangerous to ourselves and so we would not do it. Something which seems appealing because your friends are doing it, may not seem so appealing when you are alone. If you gave the situation some thought, you would realise that your body is telling you that you shouldn't do it, but you are ignoring it. You are allowing yourself to be pressured by your friends rather than make up your own mind.

Your body has certain responses in situations when you do not feel safe or comfortable. These are things such as butterflies in your tummy, nausea, trembling, sweating, hairs standing up on your neck etc. In situations when you feel these responses, it may be that your body is telling you not to take part in something. Make up your own mind and don't allow friends to pressure you into something you cannot control.

All of us have experienced group pressure at one time or another. The old adage that "If you don't do it you're a chicken" is something that your parents and grandparents will have been taunted with when they were young.

We all know how difficult it is to stand up for your views – but it is vital that you do so. Criminal or dangerous behaviour benefits no-one. It can only lead to trouble and injury. If friends are pressuring you into doing something that's wrong, you should exercise your own free choice. If your actions will harm another person in any way, **DON'T DO IT.** The victim of your actions could easily be someone close to you – maybe a relative or a friend. Would you want them to suffer?

Someone who always goes along with the crowd will never be respected. If others realise that you'll do anything they suggest, they're bound to test you to see just how far you'll go. One day you may agree to do something you'll regret. Someone could be seriously hurt or killed. It could be you.

If you are being pressured by a friend or a stranger, remember your rights; think about your safe choices. Could you explain to them that you will not join in with something just to please them? Could you walk away from them? Could you do anything else to stay safe? By using your judgement and common sense you can keep yourself feeling safe. Your friends will soon realise that standing up to them is by far the bravest thing to do. Once you have got away from the immediate pressure / danger, talk to someone you trust to make sure it doesn't happen again.

Once you have shown your friends that you're not the mindless copy-cat they imagined, you'll probably come to notice others who are not coping so well with pressure from their friends.

Don't just stand back and watch it happen – HELP!

By standing up for someone who's being pressured, you will encourage them to exercise their free choice and put over their point of view. You may be afraid of what the other members of the group will say but, when you consider what you may be preventing (i.e. pain, injury or even death), it is certainly a very small sacrifice to make.

Sometimes the pressure exerted on someone will have built up so much that there is nothing he or she can do to stop it. If someone you know is being pressured to the point of bullying, it's vital that you encourage them to tell someone they trust.

We all have the right to feel safe all of the time. Nothing is so awful that we can't tell someone about it. There is absolutely no need to live in fear of another human being.

DON'T LET IT HAPPEN!

10 Safe Choices

1. **SAY 'NO' AND MEAN 'NO'**
   Look the person in the eye
2. **BE A BROKEN RECORD**
   If you don't want to do something keep saying so
3. **DON'T RISE TO THE BAIT**
   Stay cool and collected
4. **TALK POSITIVELY ABOUT YOURSELF**
   Think of all your good points
5. **CHANGE THE SUBJECT**
   Talk about or do something else
6. **IGNORE THOSE WHO ARE TAUNTING YOU**
   They are not worth your attention
7. **AVOID THE SITUATION**
   Choose your friends carefully
8. **STAY IN A 'SAFE' GROUP**
   Remember, there's safety in numbers
9. **WALK AWAY**
   Leave temptation behind
10. **REMEMBER IT'S YOUR FREE CHOICE**
    You have the right to feel safe

On Guard!

If you see a crime being committed or notice someone acting suspiciously, note down as many details as possible.

It is important to observe calmly, discreetly and at a safe distance. This will give you the best possible chance of registering and reporting what you see quickly and accurately. Don't be afraid that you could be wasting Police time – it is better to be safe than sorry.

So long as your information is given in good faith and is as accurate as possible, the Police will be pleased to hear from you.

Here are some suggestions as to the kind of information the Police will want to know:

SUSPICIOUS PERSONS

- Male / Female
- Build
- Age
- Colour of skin
- Hair – colour, length, straight/curly/receding
- Face – long, thin, round, clean shaven moustache/beard
- Complexion
- Height
- Eye colour
- Accent – speech impediment
- Marks – scars, tattoos
- Mouth – wide, narrow
- Dress – description
- Was there an accomplice?

SUSPICIOUS VEHICLES

- Car/Van/Lorry/Motorbike
- Make/Model
- Registration Number
- Colour
- Direction of Travel
- Body Type
- Other Details: damage, company name etc.

Body Language

Body language and behavioural signs are good ways of detecting someone's intentions. You may see people doing one of many different things that makes you feel uneasy, such as looking into houses or cars, waiting outside schools, passing small packages to people, or calling at addresses.

Here are some things to look out for if you believe a person is acting suspiciously:

- ☐ Perspiring profusely
- ☐ Looking around nervously
- ☐ Trembling
- ☐ Unnatural or false smile
- ☐ Feet rooted to the floor
- ☐ Blushing
- ☐ Avoiding eye contact
- ☐ Talking hesitantly
- ☐ Voice changing unnaturally
- ☐ Fidgeting
- ☐ Long silences between words
- ☐ Overly chatty or friendly.

REMEMBER...

BY STAYING ALERT YOU CAN JOIN IN THE FIGHT AGAINST CRIME AND KEEP YOUR AREA a safer place!

Alcohol

What is alcohol?

Alcohol is made when yeast is mixed with sugary substances. The alcohol that we drink is a clear liquid called ethanol. Other types of alcohol that we cannot drink are used to make shoe polish and car de-icer sprays.

The effects

Although many people feel that alcohol stimulates them, it actually slows down the working of the brain. As the effects of alcohol take hold, the drinker begins to lose control of their body, emotions and judgement.

Alcohol, when drunk, passes from the stomach into the bloodstream travelling around the body until it reaches the brain. It is the liver that finally cleans the alcohol out of the body. Too much alcohol causes ulcers and liver damage. It also harms unborn babies.

The effects on others

We all know that too much alcohol is bad for your health, but it can also be bad for the health of others. Crimes such as drink driving, public disorder and football hooliganism are all linked to alcohol abuse. One in every three patients admitted to casualty has been drinking. Drink driving is the biggest cause of death in young men.

The Law

- At 14 you can go into a bar with an adult, but you cannot buy or drink alcoholic liquor.
- At 16 you may drink beer or cider in a pub, but only with a meal.
- At 18 you may buy alcohol, but if you drive with excess alcohol in your blood, you will lose the use of your driving licence.
- All of these are with the landlord's permission only.
- In many towns and cities it is now illegal to walk around the streets drinking alcohol.

Measures

Alcohol is measured in units but alcoholic drinks vary in strength.

One strong pint of beer contains the same amount of alcohol as about 2½ pints of ordinary beer, or just over four whiskies (pub measures).

Limits are discussed using these units, but as well as the varying strengths of drinks, different people are affected differently by alcohol.

Smaller framed people will be able to drink less before being affected, whilst people with more fat tissue absorb the alcohol into their blood stream faster, and so are also affected more quickly.

There are no hard and fast rules for alcohol. It is a drug and should be treated with care.

Here are some points of view concerning alcohol. Read through them and use your free choice to make your own decision on the subject.

POINTS OF VIEW

- At the proper time, and in moderation, adults drinking alcohol is fine.
- Getting drunk and behaving badly is just plain stupid and a waste of money.
- Drinking too much makes you unattractive to the opposite sex.
- To pretend to be 18 to get served isn't clever – it could result in a licensee losing his or her licence.
- Driving is very badly affected by drink, even by very small amounts of alcohol.
- Never accept a lift from someone who's been drinking.
- The Police are always looking out for drink drivers.
- The chances of getting caught are high and the penalties severe.
- Alcohol takes away your choice, control and your judgement.

Drugs

Drugs and the Law

Do you understand the difference between possessing and supplying drugs? Supply does not have to involve large amounts of drugs, and the penalties for supplying are far more severe than for personal possession. For example, if a small group of people pool money and one of them goes off to buy a small amount of drugs for the group that person could be prosecuted for supplying drugs. It would also be supplying drugs where a person simply gives a share to a friend to use. If a person "looks after" drugs for another person and then hands them back, if that was a Class A drug such as Ecstasy they could face a prison sentence.

Offences under The Mis-use of Drugs Act and The Drugs Trafficking Offences Act include:

- Possession.
- Possessing with intent to supply.
- Production and cultivation.
- Supplying or offering to supply.
- Importing and exporting.
- Allowing your premises to be used for supplying or offering to supply.

Drugs are divided into classes A, B and C according to how harmful they are considered. Class A, the most harmful, includes Cocaine, Ecstasy, LSD and Heroin. Class B includes Amphetamines and Barbiturates, and Class C includes Herbal Cannabis, Cannabis Resin, Benzodiazepine tranquillisers and Anabolic Steroids.

By injecting some substances, they can become Class A, and so you could become liable for more serious offences. It is important to note that you will never know exactly what you are getting for your money. Often Class B drugs will be mixed with Class A. The resulting effect could then put you in more danger.

A Conviction

Depending on the type of drug involved, a young person in particular may be given a Police warning or Formal Caution. This is a matter of discretion for the Police and would depend on all of the circumstances of the case... **BUT**, many people do not realise that if a person is sent to court for possession of a small amount of Cannabis (which many people consider to be a minor offence) and punished (even a small fine), this conviction for a drugs offence can bar them from many jobs, especially those involving work with children or young people.

Here are some examples of maximum penalties for drug offences:

	POSSESSION	PRODUCTION	TRAFFICKING
class **A** drug	7 years + unlimited Fines	Life + unlimited Fines	Life + unlimited Fines
class **B** drug	5 years + unlimited Fines	14 years + unlimited Fines	14 years + unlimited Fines
class **C** drug	2 years + unlimited Fines	14 years + unlimited Fines	14 years + unlimited Fines

Drugs and the Law

POSSESSION

S2 Mis-use of Drugs Act, 1971

IT IS AN OFFENCE TO

↓

UNLAWFULLY

Regulations define the persons who may have lawful possession, e.g. Police Constables, Post Office, Customs & Excise, etc.

↓

POSSESS

Includes things subject to his control but in the possession of another. 'Control' means knowledge of its control or shutting the eyes to the obvious.

↓

A CONTROLLED DRUG

Possession of a quantity too minute to smoke or have any effect will not justify a conviction.

↓

OR SUPPLY A CONTROLLED DRUG TO ANOTHER

THIS IS AN ARRESTABLE OFFENCE

SUPPLY

S4(3) Mis-use of Drugs Act, 1971

IT IS AN OFFENCE TO

↓

UNLAWFULLY

To be lawful it must be authorised by regulations

↓

SUPPLY Including distributing	**OFFER TO SUPPLY**
OR	**OR**
BE CONCERNED IN THE SUPPLYING OF	**BE CONCERNED IN THE MAKING OF AN OFFER TO SUPPLY**
It must be proved that it was a controlled drug. Mere belief is not sufficient.	It is not necessary to prove that it was a controlled drug. The offence is complete as soon as the offer is made.

↓

A CONTROLLED DRUG TO ANOTHER

THIS IS AN ARRESTABLE OFFENCE

Drugs and your health

We have all read stories about first time users dying unexpectedly. We hear less stories about long term illnesses - both physical and mental, but they are more common than you think. Short and long-term drug taking can seriously damage your health and we do not yet know all the long term effects and often won't until it's too late. Besides the unpleasant immediate effects of headaches, nausea and vomiting, drugs can cause long-term organ damage and eventual death. There are also the added dangers of AIDS, HIV and Hepatitis. It is common knowledge that HIV can be transmitted through sharing syringes or needles with someone who already has the virus.

Before you decide to say 'yes' to drugs, ask yourself if you are prepared to risk your life just so the person who is offering you the drugs won't think that you're a 'chicken'. Many dealers are only interested in money and your friends may only be interested in getting you involved with them. Your life comes a poor second.

Ask yourself what right you have to put your family through the pain and suffering of having a drug user in the family. We have all read stories about first-time drug users dying unexpectedly.

REMEMBER –
IT COULD HAPPEN TO YOU!

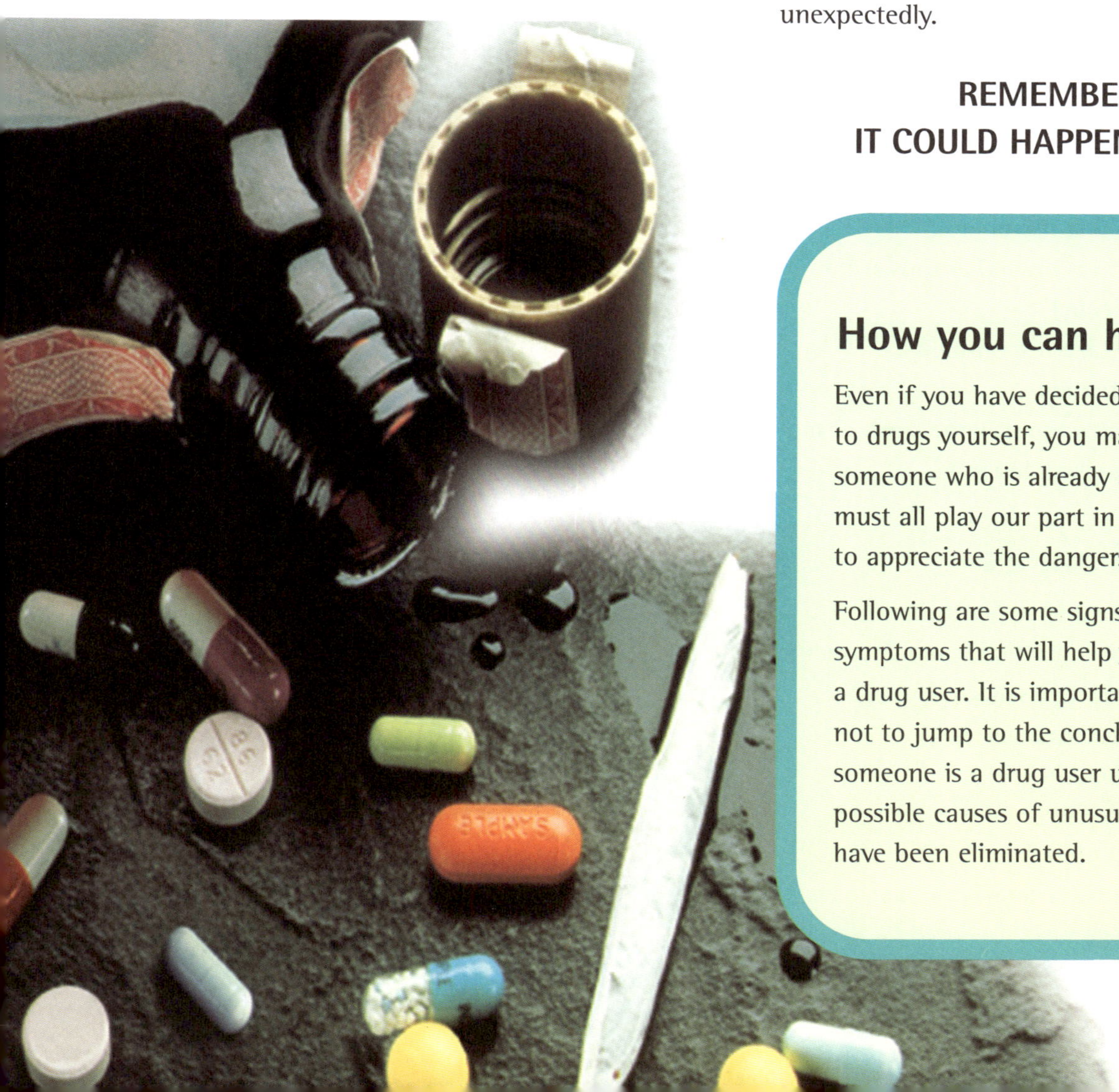

How you can help...

Even if you have decided to say **'NO'** to drugs yourself, you may well know someone who is already a user. We must all play our part in helping others to appreciate the dangers of drugs.

Following are some signs and symptoms that will help you to detect a drug user. It is important, however, not to jump to the conclusion that someone is a drug user until all other possible causes of unusual behaviour have been eliminated.

Drugs and your health

Physical Symptoms

- Drunken appearance (swaying from side to side, slurred speech etc.)
- Bloodshot or red eyes.
- Unusual eye movements.
- Very pale complexion.
- Odd speech patterns and vocabulary patterns.
- Appetite swings.
- Unexplained weight loss.
- Neglect of personal appearance.
- Becomes aggressive.
- Drowsy or sleepy.

Behavioural changes

- Moodiness, anxiety, depression, irritability.
- Over-reaction to mild criticism or simple requests.
- Introverted behaviour.
- Lack of interest in hobbies.
- Loss of motivation and enthusiasm.
- Lethargy (sleepy).
- Inability to take responsibility.
- Change in friends.
- Sudden possession of large sums of money.
- Becomes involved in crime.

School changes

- Decline in academic performance.
- Reduced concentration, span and memory.
- Loss of interest in school.
- Frequent absenteeism.
- Less participation.
- Sleeping in class.
- Behavioural problems.
- Disappearance of money or valuables.
- Untidy appearance.

Helping them to make the right choice

Once you and your friends have the correct information, then you can make an informed choice about your life.

Drugs Information

CANNABIS

SLANG TERMS:

Cannabis Resin (Hash, Hashish, Draw, Blow, Dope, Wacky-Backy) is a green/brown block of compressed resin, prepared for smoking by heating and crumbling into a pipe or a joint (spliff).

Herbal Cannabis (Marijuana, Grass, Bush, Weed, Pot, Ganja, Skunk, Weed, Sensi, Homegrown) is the leaves and flowers from a mature female cannabis plant.

USAGE:

Usually smoked either by itself or with tobacco in a joint or pipe. Sometimes eaten or used as a cooking ingredient.

EFFECTS:

Depends on mood and expectation. Relaxed, talkative, giggling, intoxication, increased appetite.

POSSIBLE RISKS:

Psychological dependency, respiratory disease, reduced co-ordination and reaction. Short term memory loss, anxiety, panic attacks, mental illness.

ECSTASY

SLANG TERMS:

E's, Brownies, Fantasy, Adam, Discs, Biscuits, Love Dove, Phase Four, New Yorkers, Discoburgers, White Doves, Dennis the Menace, Rhubarb and Custard, Cities and United.

USAGE:

Swallowed (Tablets of various colours). Heavy users might try to inject.

EFFECTS:

Increased energy, euphoria, nausea, calmness, drop in anger and hostility. Effects start 20-60 minutes after taking and can last for several hours.

POSSIBLE RISKS:

Impure tablets, panic, anxiety and confusion, fatigue, depression, irregular temperature control.

ASSOCIATED RISKS:

Dehydration, exhaustion, collapse, coma, death.

LONG TERM EFFECTS:

They are not known as widespread use is recent.

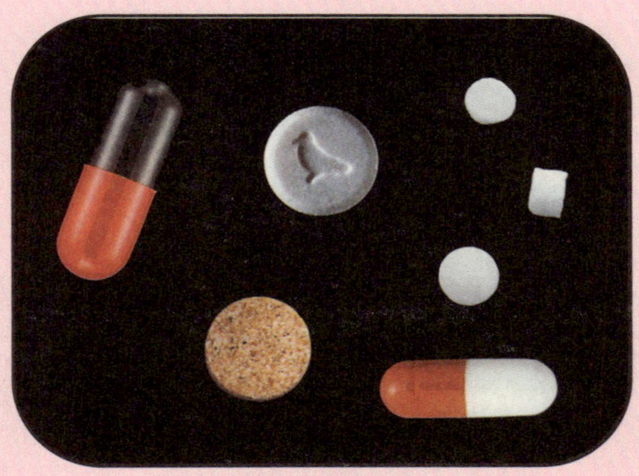

Drugs Information

LSD LYSERGIC ACID DIETHYLAMIDE

■ **SLANG TERMS:**
LSD Strawbs, Acid, Trips, Tabs, Blotters, Domes, Flats and Barrels, Stars, Smilies, Strawberries, Penguins, Micro Dots and many more.

■ **USAGE:**
LSD can come dropped onto a sugar cube, capsules, in gelatin sheets or strips, tablets and on blotting paper. Now usually distributed on 5mm squares of blotting paper that includes a printed image.

■ **EFFECTS:**
Depends on the mood at the time of taking and the dosage. Visual distortion, mystical experiences. Trip begins 30 to 60 minutes after taking and lasts up to 12 hours depending on the strength of dose.

■ **POSSIBLE RISKS:**
Disturbing experiences during bad trips, accidents, flashbacks. Can trigger underlying mental health problems and produce delusions and paranoia. The long term effects are not really fully known.

HEROIN

■ **SLANG TERMS:**
Smack, Skag, Gear, Boy, Brown, 'H', Junk, Henry, Harry, Horse, Jack, Elephant, 765.

■ **USAGE:**
Sniffed (Chasing the Dragon), smoked or prepared for injection. Other heroin-type drugs may be in tablet or liquid form and taken orally or prepared for injection.

■ **EFFECTS:**
Euphoria, drowsiness, slurred speech, relieves stress and discomfort, feeling of well being. Effects can last for several hours.

■ **POTENTIAL DISADVANTAGES:**
Physical dependence and tolerance. Appetite is suppressed and the body dehydrates. Nausea, vomiting, constipation, and a risk of overdose with potentially fatal consequences, poor dental hygiene (decreased ability to recognise pain). Impaired ability to make decisions about safer sex or about behaviour.

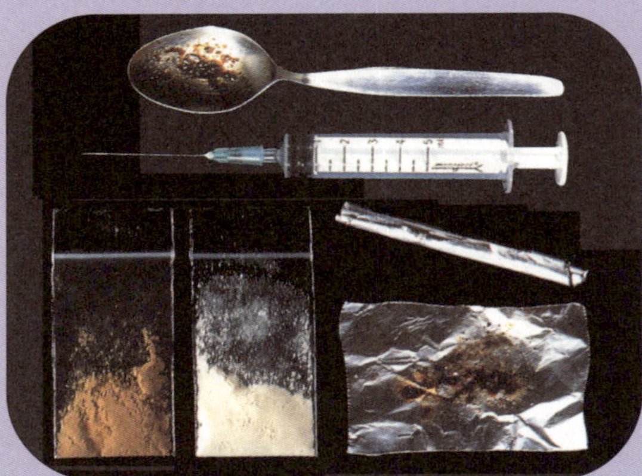

COCAINE

SLANG TERMS:
Coke, Snow, C, Charlie, Nose Candy, Dust, Gold Dust, Lady, White.

USAGE:
A white powder that can be snorted up the nose using a straw or a bank note. It is sometimes prepared for injection.

EFFECTS:
Increased alertness, euphoria, increased pulse rate and blood pressure, energetic, confident, feeling of strength. Strong stimulant drug with short lived effects up to 30 minutes, users are often left craving more.

POSSIBLE RISKS:
Physiological and psychological dependency, panic, anxiety, irritability, psychosis, poor impulse control leading to increased aggression, impaired decision making may lead to high risk sexual behaviour (H.I.V., Hep. B., Hep. C.). Snorting cocaine may permanently damage the inside of the nose.

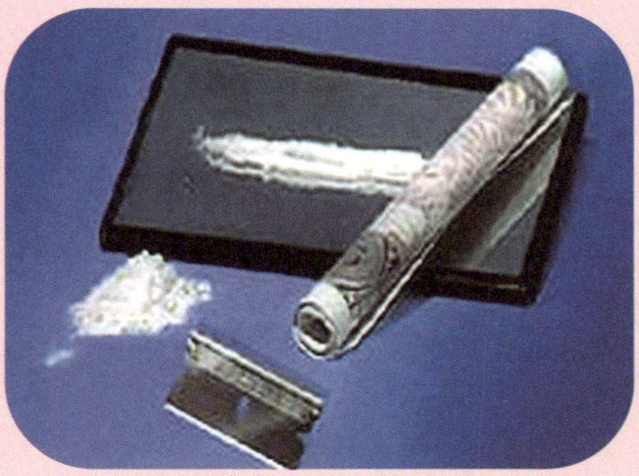

CRACK

SLANG TERMS:
Rock, Freebase, Wash, Stone, Base, Flake, Gravel, Ice.

USAGE:
Crack is a smokeable form of cocaine. Smoked in special pipes, flattened cans, tubes or bottles. Very quick effect. Euphoria lasts for 10-12 minutes.

EFFECTS:
Euphoria, feeling of well being, increased confidence, increased sexual libido, feeling strong or powerful. Decrease in appetite.

POTENTIAL DISADVANTAGES:
Wheezy chest (change of voice), chest pains, coughs, sore throats, chest infections, overdose with potential fatal consequences. Panic / anxiety, psychosis, poor impulse control leading to increased aggression, hostility, psychological dependency.

Drugs Information

BARBITURATES

SLANG TERMS:
Barbs, Barbies, Blues, Bullets, Sleepers, Nembies, Devils.

USAGE:
By mouth or prepared for injection.

EFFECTS:
Strong depressant. Slows mental and physical functioning. In small quantities helps people to relax. In larger doses effects are like being drunk. High doses sedate, resulting in loss of co-ordination and sleep.

POSSIBLE RISKS:
Increased risk of accidents. High doses may make people very aggressive. Significant risk of fatal overdose. The lethal dose is close to the normal dose level. Physical dependence and tolerance can develop quickly with regular use. Heavy users may suffer health problems including bronchitis and pneumonia and can have severe withdrawal symptoms.

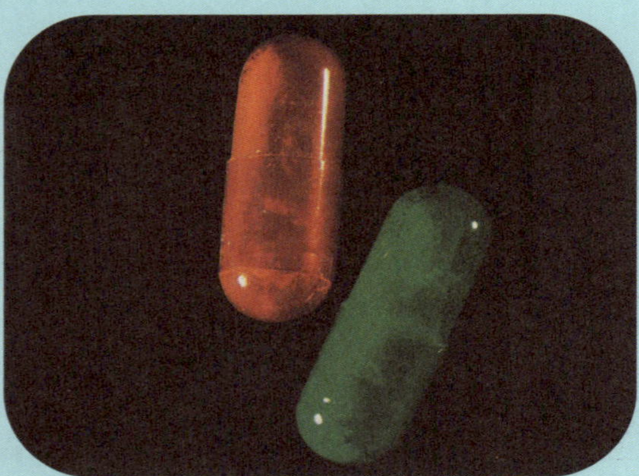

MAGIC MUSHROOMS

SLANG TERMS:
Liberties, 'Shrooms, Mushies.

USAGE:
Eaten raw or after being dried out. Sometimes used as cooking ingredient or made into a tea.

EFFECTS:
Hallucinogenic drug with similar effects to LSD, but usually milder. It depends on the user's mood, some people laugh a lot, some have stomach pains and vomiting. High doses result in a 'trip' with distortions of vision and hearing. Effects can last up to six hours depending on how many are taken.

POSSIBLE RISKS:
Some people experience a 'bad trip' - feeling paranoid and/or sick which is likely if they already feel anxious. As with LSD, there is no risk of physical dependence, tolerance or fatal overdose, but flashbacks can occur. Picking the wrong mushroom can result in poisoning.

SOLVENTS

SLANG TERMS:
Glue, Gas, Aero, Bute.

USAGE:
Vapours are inhaled through the nose and/or mouth. Directly inhaled or put in a bag, on a rag or squirted up a sleeve before sniffing.

EFFECTS:
A bit like getting drunk very quickly. Breathing and heart rate slow, and users feel light-headed and sometimes drowsy and unsteady on their feet. Effects start quickly but wear off in less than an hour without a repeat dose.

POSSIBLE RISKS:
Abusing gases, glues or aerosols can lead to nausea, vomiting, black-outs and fatal heart problems, long-term abuse damages the brain, liver and kidneys. There is a risk of suffocation if the substance is inhaled from a plastic bag over the head. About 150 young people a year die using solvents.

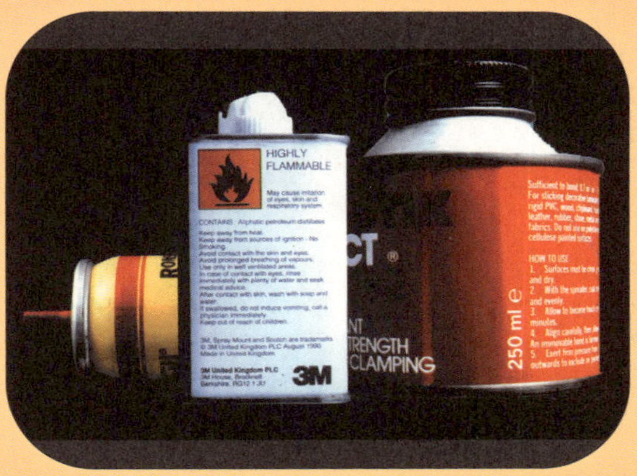

TRANQUILLISERS

SLANG TERMS:
Benzos, Tranx, Moggies (Mogadon), Mazzies (Temazepam), Diazepam, Nitrazepam.

USAGE:
Tablets and pills are usually taken orally. Temazepam can be prepared for injection.

EFFECTS:
Depressant drugs. Slow mental and physical functioning. Shut out feelings. Make people calmer and less anxious. Large doses make people feel drowsy, lethargic, forgetful and sleepy.

POSSIBLE RISKS:
Tolerance can develop quickly so that increasing doses are needed, users become dependent, especially if they rely on the drug to calm them or help them to sleep. Withdrawal can lead to anxiety, headaches, nausea and confusion. After regular high doses sudden withdrawal can lead to fits. Extremely dangerous if mixed with alcohol.

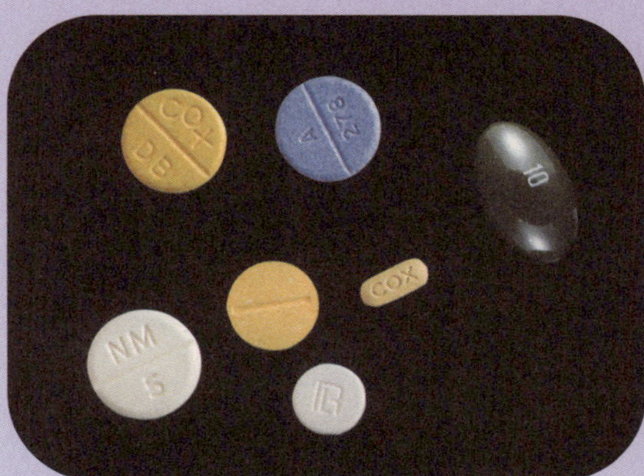

Drugs Information

AMPHETAMINES

SLANG TERMS:
Speed, Whizz, Amph, Sulphate, Billy, Fast, Uppers.

USAGE:
A grey, white or dirty-white powder usually swallowed in a drink, sniffed up the nose or eaten in a wrap. Tablets taken by mouth. Sometimes prepared for injection.

EFFECTS:
Stimulant, making people feel more awake, alert and confident, reducing the need to sleep and eat. It quickens the heart beat and breathing rate. Single dose may last 3-4 hours. May make some people feel very anxious and restless. As the effects wear off, people may feel very tired and sometimes depressed.

POSSIBLE RISKS:
Regular users may feel very low when the effects wear off and be tempted to take more. Tolerance and dependence can develop with regular use. Depression, violent mood swings, aggressive behaviour and paranoia can occur.

NITRATES POPPERS

SLANG TERMS:
Liquid Gold, Amyl, Butyl, Poppers, Ram, Rush, Snapper, Stag, Stud, Thrust, TNT, Ruah, Stud, Locker Room, .

USAGE:
Gold-coloured liquids which usually come in small bottles, the vapours from the liquid are inhaled through the nose or mouth.

EFFECTS:
Users get a brief but intense 'head-rush', caused by a sudden surge of blood through the heart and brain, which results in a flushed face and neck. Effects fade 2-5 minutes after use.

POSSIBLE RISKS:
Can make people feel faint and sick, users often experience a headache afterwards. Very dangerous for people with anaemia, glaucoma, heart or blood pressure problems. Poppers may be fatal if swallowed.

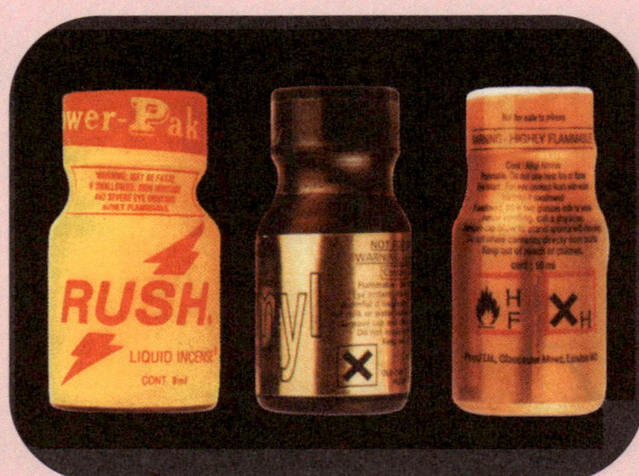

ANABOLIC STEROIDS

SLANG TERMS:
Roids, Juice, Stuff, Sustanon 250, Deca-Durabolin, Dianabol, Anavar, Stanozolol.

USAGE:
Swallowed as pills or capsules or sometimes injected.

EFFECTS:
Build up body weight and increase muscle size. May make people more aggressive and competitive.

POSSIBLE RISKS:
Taking steroids carries many health risks and can stop young people from growing properly. It is also associated with abnormal growth for both men and women. Particularly dangerous if injected into veins.

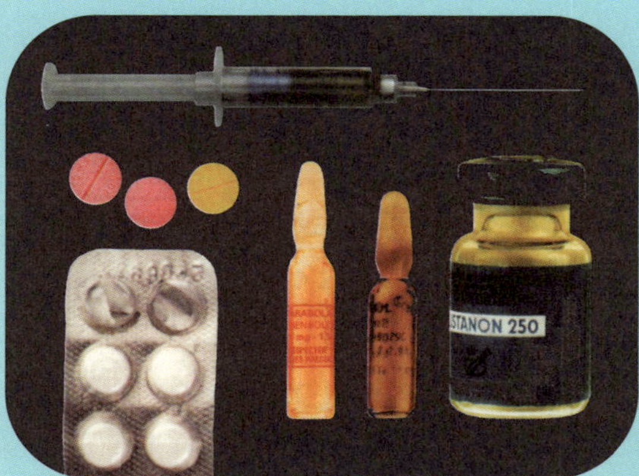

KETAMINE

SLANG TERMS:
Special K, Vitamin K, K.

USAGE:
Ketamine is sometimes sold as ecstasy. It can come as white powder that can be snorted, a liquid that can be injected or a tablet that can be swallowed.

EFFECTS:
Makes users feel that the mind has been separated from the body, creates an 'out of body' and hallucinatory experience for up to 3 hours. Like LSD the effects are influenced by the user's mood and environment. The user may be physically unable to move.

POSSIBLE RISKS:
As Ketamine numbs the body, users risk serious injury without feeling pain. Excessive doses carry some risk of breathing problems and heart failure. Very dangerous when mixed with alcohol and other drugs.

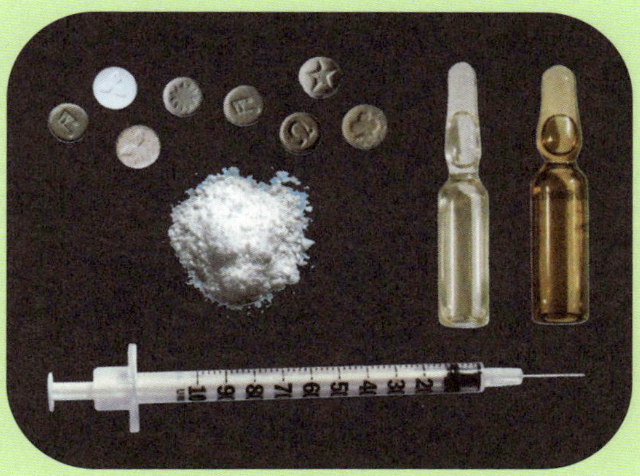

Drugs Information

CAFFEINE

USAGE:
Occurs naturally in tea, coffee and cocoa plants. Contained in many soft drinks, for example colas. Swallowed in drinks or eaten in confectionery.

EFFECTS:
Mild stimulant which increases heart rate and blood pressure. Makes people more alert and less tired. Effects start quickly and can last a few hours. Makes people urinate more. Large amounts may make people edgy and give them headaches.

POSSIBLE RISKS:
Regular use (6-8 cups of tea/coffee a day) often leads to dependency but this is not usually regarded as a problem. May increase insomnia. Stopping intake often leads to withdrawal symptoms (tiredness, headaches, edginess). Some reports say that heavy, long-term use may increase risk of peptic ulcers and kidney, bladder, heart and blood pressure problems.

GHB

SLANG TERMS:
Short for Gammahydroxybutyrate. Also known as GBH, Liquid E, Fantasy.

USAGE:
GHB comes as a colourless liquid and is sold in small bottles or capsules. The liquid is measured out in capfuls and then swallowed. It has no smell but a salty taste. It can also come in powder form, which is then dissolved in water and swallowed.

EFFECTS:
GHB has sedative properties and can produce feelings of euphoria. Effects have been known to last for a day.

POSSIBLE RISKS:
Excessive hits could lead to sickness, stiff muscles, fits and even collapse. If incorrectly produced, it can badly burn the mouth and is very dangerous when mixed with alcohol or other drugs. High doses can cause dizziness, nausea, vomiting, muscle spasm, loss of consciousness and coma.

Helping others to make the right choice...

Once you and your friends have the correct information, you can then make an informed choice.

There's nothing worse than talking to someone who simply refuses to listen. But no matter how irritating the situation becomes, it is vital that you don't act aggressively. Remember, the drug user is a victim. He or she needs help – not accusation.

One of the best ways of preparing yourself to talk to a user is to put yourself in their position. Think of the arguments you have with your parents about staying out late, smoking or drinking. What approach do they take when they're persuading you not to do something?

Here are some approaches that usually don't work. They tend to get people's backs up and inflate the situation.

- **SARCASM:** "I suppose behaving like that makes you a responsible adult"
- **ACCUSATION:** "That's a downright lie!"
- **STIGMATISING:** "You're a cruel, deceitful, self-centred child!"
- **SYMPATHY-SEEKING:** "After all I've done for you."
- **SELF-BLAMING:** "I suppose I've only got myself to blame for giving you so much of your own way when you were younger."
- **POSSESSIVE:** "Whilst you're living under this roof you'll do as I say."
- **THREATENING:** "Just wait till your father hears about this."
- **INFALLIBILITY:** "Because I say so."
- **CAUSING EMBARRASSMENT:** "I know what you've been up to. I've been 14 as well you know."

Now that we've highlighted the techniques that don't work, here are some approaches you should use.

First of all, calm down and approach the situation reasonably.

1. Put the person at their ease straight away.
2. Be a good listener.
3. Don't prejudge the person.
4. Look at positive aspects of the person (praise them for their good points).
5. Explain why drugs are bad for them.
6. Tell them all of the things they have to live for.
7. Put yourself in their situation
8. Be firm and positive: "We will beat it!".
9. Be supportive: "I'll help you!".
10. Talk to them about your bad points – don't just focus on theirs.
11. Be a constant feature of their lives – be there for them all the time.
12. Show how happy you are, i.e. drugs are not vital to a happy life.

If you need further help or advice, please contact the NATIONAL DRUGS HELPLINE:

0800 776600

By helping someone overcome their addiction you could be saving their life

'My Great Escape'

THE REAL LIFE EXPERIENCE OF VANYA BROWN, A TEENAGER WHO ALMOST DIED AS A RESULT OF DRUG ABUSE.

"I'd had a real rough time of it when I came across my escape plan. I wasn't doing well at school. I'd been suspended several times after skipping lessons, smoking in school, well – you know the sort of things I'm on about.

I wasn't getting on well with my family at home and the atmosphere there was unbearable at times. Anyway, about my 'escape plan', as I call it. I just happened to stumble across it one day. I overheard two girls talking, saying that they'd had enough and needed to 'cheer up'. As the conversation continued, I began to realise that they were talking about drugs, specifically acid (LSD). Anyway, me being me, plus how I was feeling at the time, I decided to get involved and that's how it began. I starting smoking cannabis and then progressed to acid. This went on for seven or eight months. It was my escape from the reality of the world, which for me was too much to cope with. Now with the drugs, I thought that I could do anything!!

That was until I came 'down'. When the effects wore off, I would have to get some more acid. It was a vicious circle – up, down, up, down – and I became extremely happy, but extremely moody. In the end I was taking five or six acid tabs in one go on top of drinking and smoking. I stayed out overnight, not telling my family where I was going or what I was up to.

In amongst all this, I started seeing a lad who, although he was dead against drugs, stood by me. He lectured me about the dangers all the time, but I didn't care. I'd taken them for ages and they hadn't done me any harm – yet!

A few of my friends were going to have an 'All Night Party' in the middle of nowhere. I decided that it would be great fun, a laugh, so I looked forward to a really good night. My boyfriend said it was going to be a drug-free party and told me to behave, but I wasn't having any of it. I invited a couple of similarly minded friends who brought along some acid tabs, cannabis and some magic mushrooms.

When I got there, after a really long walk, my boyfriend was already there. He had set up a tent and had lit a fire. As he sorted the drinks out, my friends and I settled down and had a 'smoke', ate some of the mushrooms and popped some acid tabs into our mouths. After about ten minutes, I still hadn't felt the effects of the drugs so I took some more! I started to feel dizzy, but that's not unusual. However, I knew something was wrong. As I stood up to go to the tent, I could hear my heart beating and I started to breathe heavily. I then collapsed. I remember my boyfriend saying, "Don't be stupid, get up." I tried to reply, to tell him that something was wrong. I was scared but I could do little more than mumble. I saw someone lean over me and heard them say, "She's really tripping, look at her eyes." My boyfriend picked me up and carried me to his car which was parked some distance away, only to find that the people I'd gone to the party with had, prior to running away, slit the tyres to prevent us from getting to the hospital (and being subsequently questioned by the authorities). Fortunately, an ambulance was called and the next thing I knew, I was in the back of it, then in hospital with a doctor and nurses running all around me.

When I regained consciousness, I found myself in intensive care. I was surrounded with the wires and tubes and aware of the 'beep beeps' of various machines. I wasn't really sure of what was happening. I tried to talk but I couldn't. I tried to move but I couldn't. I became aware that I couldn't feel anything – all I could do was cry.

A few days later, I was moved to a room of my own on one of the wards. Then, for the next three months, I slowly had to learn to walk/talk/hold a pen/feed myself and go to the toilet all over again. I kept getting the shakes, wetting myself and stuttering. It was all very frightening. When I could talk enough for people to understand me, I asked the doctors what had happened. To this day, they're still not sure but they believe that I had an allergic reaction to one of the drugs. They added that one in three tabs contain the same thing that made me collapse – one in three! Apparently, I'd stopped breathing at the party, then again in the ambulance. I 'died' three times in hospital. My 'escape plan' had brought me back down to earth with a bump!

Drugs nearly killed me. It was only the actions of my boyfriend that got me some help or I wouldn't be here today. You may think that 'it won't happen to me' – well that's what I thought! But my temporary escape became a prison that I nearly didn't get out of. Even when I did, reality was still reality. We all make mistakes and my biggest one ever was drugs. I'm now married with a baby girl of nine months, and well aware that life is worth living. My 'escape plan' nearly killed me, I was lucky – you may not be."

Solvent Abuse

"Sniffing isn't exciting, it's just bloody stupid."

DARREN, AN EX-SOLVENT ABUSER

In 2001 sniffing cost 63 lives – that's over five deaths a month. Most of the deaths were in the 14-18 age group. Sniffing can affect the heart, cause swelling of throat tissues or suffocation. Some solvents contain poisonous substances, others are a fire risk.
Sniffing makes your clothes and breath smell – it also causes spots.

Some young people sniff solvents instead of drinking alcohol. They feel that the element of danger in solvent abuse is more exciting than drinking. Solvents are cheap and readily available in most households. Abusers get hooked on the hallucinations which result from their habit. These can often be dangerous, unpleasant and frightening.

Although many of the symptoms of solvent abuse have been discussed in our section on illegal drug abuse, here are some specific tell-tale signs of solvent abuse:

- Chemical smells on clothes or breath.
- Unusual marks around nose and mouth.
- Frequent and persistent headaches, sore throat or runny nose.

Under the Intoxicating Substances Supply Act (1985) it is an offence to supply a person under 18 with a substance that the supplier believes will be used to achieve intoxication.

READ THE FOLLOWING PAGES ABOUT THE RESULTS OF SOLVENT ABUSE AND THEN MAKE UP YOUR OWN MIND ON THE SUBJECT.

POINTS OF VIEW

- It's a dangerous, stupid habit that kills many young people each year.
- Sniffing aerosols can kill at the first attempt.
- Sniffing can affect the heart.
- The number of solvent mis-use-related deaths rose from 2 in 1971 to 63 in 2001.
- Hallucinations caused by sniffing can be dangerous, unpleasant and frightening.

REMEMBER – you could be saving someone's life.

Reproduced by kind permission of Salisbury Journal Newspapers.

Teenagers are dicing with death

SHOCKING proof of potentially lethal solvent abuse has been discovered in public toilets in the heart of Fordingbridge where teenagers gather at night.

By Bob Jolliffe

Cleaners have found apparatus used in connection with solvent abuse, including an empty fire extinguisher and a milk bottle with a plastic tube.

The finds in the public loos at Roundhill have led to a dire warning to parents from the town's police sergeant John Williams.

Inhaling glue and other chemicals can kill or cause brain damage, he said.

Last November, Ringwood teenager John Paul Davison died after sniffing butane gas from a bottle while on a fishing trip at Hucklesbrook Lakes. Attempts to resuscitate him failed and he was dead on arrival at Salisbury District Hospital.

"Parents ought to be aware there is a problem of youngsters congregating and we have found evidence that glue sniffing has been taking place," said Sgt Williams.

"We want parents to be on their guard and keep an eye on their children's activities."

Up to 40 young people aged between 12 and 16 regularly gather at the Roundhill end of the main car park.

"It may be totally unconnected with the group that is congregating. This may be happening later at night when the youngsters have all gone home," said Sgt Williams.

"Youngsters are entitled to congregate together and, provided they do not commit an offence, there's nothing in law that can, or should, be done about it."

Police will now step up their patrols in the area and Sgt Williams is visiting the car park in the evenings.

He wants to meet Burgate School head teacher Celia Nicholls to see what can be done about the problem.

"I will also try and get the council to close the toilets at night.

"The youngsters are unlikely to do it in the public view but giving them a place to go and hide in is not an ideal situation."

How you can help...

If you know someone who is a solvent abuser, try to talk to them about it or suggest that they talk to somebody about it. Explain that they can have a good time without solvents, tell them how solvents can damage their health and make sure that tempting aerosols, glues and gas canisters are kept well out of their way.

By finding new and exciting experiences for the abuser you will help them to kick their habit. Sniffing is often the result of a deeper problem. It is important that you try to get to the bottom of these problems by talking to the abuser.

If you feel that you are out of your depth advising an abuser then suggest other people they can seek help from, including professionals. The abuser may not want to speak to someone in authority themselves, so why not offer to act as mediator for them?

READ THIS NEWSPAPER EXTRACT CAREFULLY, THEN ASK IF YOU WANT TO RISK YOUR LIFE.

VICTIMS OF SNIFFING LIGHTER FUEL

Two Fife Teenagers die in one week

By Clair Warrender

A FIFE father has told of his family's utter devastation at the loss of their only son, who died last week after sniffing butane gas.

Sixteen-year-old apprentice butcher Lee O'Brien was found dead on Wednesday by his girlfriend Gina, who is two months pregnant with his child.

She discovered his body in the kitchen of her Methil flat, which Lee had been decorating in preparation for the birth of their baby and where he was planning to live with them.

Lee's father John said the family had taken some comfort from the fact that Gina (19) had promised to call the baby Lee whether it was a boy or a girl, and said "It means I'll still have part of Lee."

Lee's death was the second such tragedy to hit Fife last week, coming just days after an 18-year-old student was found dead at his Kirkcaldy home. He had also been inhaling lighter fuel.

Confirmation of both incidents prompted Lee's father to speak out in a bid to prevent another fatality.

"I don't want any more victims. If my son is sacrificed to save others then so be it," he said.

"This has had a devastating affect on our family. His two sisters, Susan and Lorna, are both devastated and I don't see the point in pushing this aside.

"This sort of thing is rife out there in the streets and young people don't seem to realise the dangers.

"The quicker this is brought out in the open and brought to people's attention the better, then Lee won't have died for nothing."

A former pupil of both Inverkeithing and Kirkland high schools, Lee lived with his mother Lynne in Dalgety Bay until 18 months ago, when he moved to be with his father in Turner Crescent, Methil.

He started a new job just a fortnight ago at Weepers' butchers shop in Kirkcaldy and John said he was highly regarded by his bosses.

However, he added that his son was still young and easily influenced, commenting, "When he moved to Methil he wanted to make friends but he was easily led. I don't think he did this sort of thing all the time. As far as I know it was only the second time he had done it and it killed him."

He said Lee had told Gina he was going to a local shop to buy chewing gum but actually bought the fatal dose of butane gas.

Gina discovered his body when she returned from collecting her two-year-old daughter from nursery.

John added, "Gina comes round here all the time and she's a really nice girl. This is bound to affect her badly.

"Lee was really excited about the baby and he was looking forward to the future. I think he wanted to give himself a wee buzz because it's a lot for a boy of 16 to take in."

John and his partner Caroline O'Keefe plan to launch a campaign to persuade lighter fuel manufacturers to come up with a safety device to ensure the fluid cannot be used for anything other than filling lighters.

The deaths of two teenagers last week are just the latest in a line of shocking incidents involving butane gas and similar substances in Fife.

In July two 14-year-old west Fife boys were reported to the children's panel after being found inhaling the contents of butane gas cylinders in Dunfermline and in September two young girls - one 13 and the other just nine - were discovered inhaling solvents from a plastic bag.

Some years ago a Kirkcaldy teenager was burned to death while inhaling petrol, and in a separate tragedy a west Fife teenager was badly scarred as a result of burns sustained when the petrol she was inhaling ignited.

Fife Police yesterday warned youngsters about the dangers of sniffing substances.

"Sad as this is, we would hope this tragic waste of lives can now act as a salutary lesson for others, underlining the crazy risks that are involved in this area of abuse," said Detective Inspector Alan Small.

"Sadly, several young people still die every month in the United Kingdom from solvent abuse, many of whom are actually first time users, and we must never allow ourselves to believe that this is no longer a problem here in Fife.

"These latest incidents only serve to underline that solvent abuse is still with us and the potential for a young life to be lost remains just as scary today as it always has done."

SOLVENT ABUSE is most common among 12 to 16-year-olds and tends to go in and out of fashion.

The effects come on quickly and disappear as fast, the experience for abusers being as if they are drunk, light-headed and dizzy, dreamy or having hallucinations. Others feel sick and drowsy and the after-effects can be like a hangover.

Parents should look out for the smell of chemicals on children's breath or clothing. Habitual sniffers may appear drowsy, unco-ordinated and forgetful and their physical health may generally deteriorate. People who have been sniffing look and behave as if they are drunk and there may be personality changes.

Booklets and information for people anxious about their youngster's possible involvement are available from Fife's principal police stations.

Better to be safe than sorry

If you find someone drowsy or unconscious through alcohol, drug or solvent abuse, it is important to act correctly.

- STAY CALM...
- Make sure that the air passages are clear and remove anything in the mouth. Check the tongue has not slipped backwards, obstructing the airway.
- Loosen tight clothing around the chest and place in the recovery position (see illustration). This will prevent the person from choking if he or she is sick.
- Call a doctor or an ambulance if you are at all concerned. Tell the medics what they have taken.

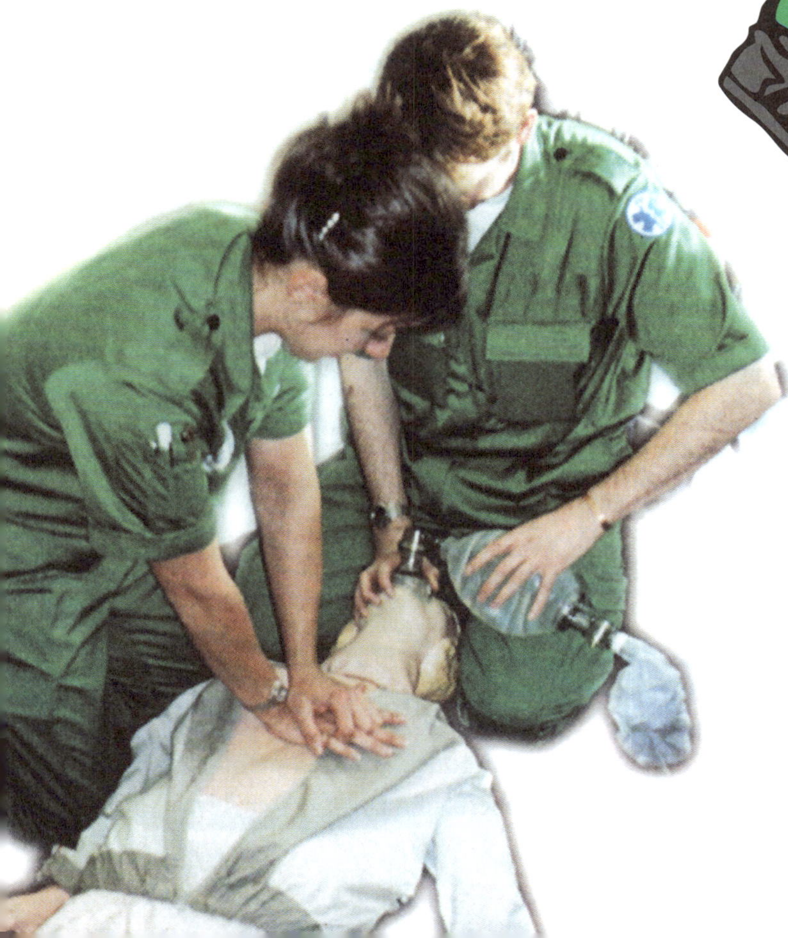

- If the person is not in such a bad way, try to stop further immediate drug use without using force.
- Stay with the person until the effects have worn off.

- **DO NOT** Excite or chase the person. If glue has been sniffed this can lead to Sudden Sniffing Death.
- **DO NOT** Try to discuss their drug or solvent abuse at this point.

How you can help...

Drug abuse is a very big issue for young people today. It is very important that you help the authorities to overcome drug problems in your area.

Here are some projects that you could set up with the help of your friends:

- Organise an anti-drugs poster competition for local schools. The winners should be given a prize and all of the entries can be used to advertise the anti-drugs campaign around your town.
- Produce and distribute leaflets warning of the dangers of drugs.
- Set up a drugs advice group to give confidential advice and guidance to parents and youngsters.

Car Crime

If you ever own your own home then a car is the second most valuable thing you will ever own. For many people it will be the most valuable! Imagine how you would feel if someone had stolen your family car. Imagine if you had to be somewhere really important and you couldn't get there because the car had gone. People need their cars for lots of reasons, even medical reasons. Imagine the chaos caused if someone takes it.

How good are you at spotting the value of an item? Well here's a chance to find out.

Q The following objects are all relatively expensive to buy, but which one is the most valuable?

A The car probably costs up to 25 times as much as any of these other valuables.

No-one with any sense would leave a diamond ring or a wad of fivers out in the open. But car owners have to leave one of their most expensive possessions by the roadside.

Very few of us would ever consider stealing someone else's money or jewellery, but cars are somehow no longer classed with other valuables. If potential car thieves realised that they are stealing an average of £5,000 from the car owner, do you think they would still class car theft as petty crime?

Make sure your family car is not the target of crime

- Encourage your relatives and friends to improve their car security by installing an immobiliser.
- Make sure that nothing valuable is left on show in the car.
- Security-mark the car's cassette or CD player.
- Always lock your car up at home.

FACTS...

- **On average a car is stolen or broken into once every 25 seconds.**
- **A stolen car is 2,000 times more likely to be involved in an accident than a legally owned vehicle.**
- **Car crime costs Britain over £3 billion a year.**
- **Less than one tenth of valuables stolen from cars are ever recovered.**

The majority of car offenders are aged 17-25 years old and most started offending between the ages of 13 and 16. Many young people are persuaded into car crime by their friends.

POINTS OF VIEW

- It isn't only the big insurance companies that pay the cost of car theft. We all do.
- Joyriding is a stupid, inconsiderate and extremely dangerous thing to get involved in.
- After their home, cars are often a person's most valuable possession.
- Car crime starts as theft and can lead to death.
- Car thefts make up almost a third of all reported crime.
- One in four of the cars reported missing each year is never recovered.

Here you'll find a newspaper article and some points of view on car theft and joyriding. Read through this article and points of view, then use your free choice to decide if it is a good idea to get involved in car crime.

Although you may not be directly involved in car crime yourself, you may know someone who is. Take time out to talk to them about their problem. Explain what the possible outcome of their actions might be and show them newspaper reports on the effects of car crime. Every year, hundreds of people are killed or injured through car crime. The victims could easily be your family or friends. By sitting back and turning a blind eye, we become partly responsible for the consequences of car crime.

Three die in joyride smash

THREE young joyriders died after the stolen car they were in left the road at 70 mph and ploughed into the wall of an elderly couple's house. A fourth is critically ill in hospital after the horror crash in Coatbridge, Lanarkshire.

The smash was so horrific that fire officers had to receive counselling at the scene after cutting the bodies free. A senior fire officer said it was the worst crash site he had attended in his 20 years with the brigade.

The driver apparently lost control of the stolen red Ford Orion as it raced down the Old Monkland Road in Coatbridge in the early hours of Saturday morning.

The vehicle turned a somersault, went airborne, crashed through fencing, tumbled down an embankment and smashed into the bedroom wall of a ground floor flat where an elderly couple in their 70s live, before bouncing back and landing on its roof.

The couple were on holiday at the time. Police officers said if they had been at home they might have been killed.

Structural engineers had to be called out to assess the damage to the block of flats. Residents were warned by workers to turn off their electricity in case of a possible gas leak.

A local councillor said he would hold urgent talks with the police to get traffic calming measures in place claiming there had been a number of recent fatalities.

Grieving friends and relatives laid floral tributes to the teenagers throughout the day. Two Celtic jerseys were fastened onto a fence with washing pegs, and a single green and white Celtic scarf was tied to a lamp post nearby.

A bouquet of pink carnations, and two further bunches of flowers marked the point where the car plunged through the security fence, before smashing into the wall.

At the scene of the crash a pile of masonry and broken glass, the car's twisted exhaust pipe caught in fencing and skid marks on the road bore testament to the severity of the smash. Damage to the flat indicates the car was four feet off the ground at the time of the impact.

The stolen car was not being pursued by police at the time of the crash.

Joyriding

JOYRIDING – WHOSE JOY???

This is a nice word for theft. Having a nice word doesn't make it any less serious.

Before you decide to turn a blind eye to joyriding, look at the following statistics:

At 40mph **MOST PEDESTRIANS ARE KILLED**

At 30mph **HALF ARE KILLED**

At 20mph **1 in 20 IS KILLED**

We can't let the killing continue. Say 'NO' to joyriding!

How you can help...

Car Crime is the fastest rising crime in the country and, as such, we need to give it some serious attention.

HERE ARE SOME PROJECT IDEAS:

- Carry out a car crime survey with the help of residents in your local area.
- Perform an anti-car crime play and hold workshops in local primary schools.
- Discuss the possibilities of setting up motor projects to enable your friends to learn about machinery safety and the danger of car crime.
- Produce a video warning of the dangers of joyriding.
- Make car security a priority with your family!

CAR CRIME
TOGETHER WE'LL CRACK IT

Bullying

What is bullying?

Bullying is very hard to define. We've all come across the big surly school bully at some time, but it isn't only those who are obviously aggressive that bully others. Bullying often takes the form of laughing at someone or having fun at their expense.

People who bully are usually very insecure. They feel the need to prove their strength through emphasising someone else's weakness. Bullies make out that their bullying is the victim's fault. **THIS IS NOT TRUE.**

Have you ever been a bully?

If you have ever played any part in bullying someone, it is vital that you understand the full consequences of your actions. Put yourself in the position of the victim. Would you enjoy being laughed at or picked on?

Here are some newspaper extracts (overleaf) and points of view which examine the consequences of bullying. Read through these and then ask yourself, "Is bullying such a good idea?"

POINTS OF VIEW

- Bullies are usually very insecure people.
- Don't be afraid to be yourself.
- Everyone should live and let live.
- Bullying is often a sign of jealousy.
- Bullying is never the victim's fault.

HERE ARE SOME NEWSPAPER EXTRACTS ABOUT BULLYING. READ THEM CAREFULLY.

School bullying 'has long-term effect on victims'

ONE IN FIVE children either bullies other pupils or is bullied, according to one of the most extensive surveys of school behaviour in Britain.

The research, funded by the Department for Education, will be completed by the end of the year. It is intended that all schools will then be provided with comprehensive advice on how to combat the problem.

Professor Peter Smith, of the Department of Psychology at Sheffield University, said yesterday that about a dozen cases of bullying every year are so extreme that they result in teenagers taking their own lives. Some victims are as young as 10 or 11 years old.

He told the annual meeting in Oxford yesterday of the Social Psychology Section of the British Psychological Society: "Bullying is not a trivial thing. The suicides are the tip of the iceberg. Many children suffer, making them unhappy children and under-achievers.

"There is evidently a long-term effect with more depression in adult life and people finding it harder to form adult relationships," he said

Professor Smith said that bullies were more likely than other children to see the world as a hard place and to interpret the actions of others as aggressive.

He found that 44 per cent of bullies felt that they were picked on compared with 12 per cent of non-bullies.

The survey - of 24 schools, involving 7,000 pupils - found that 27 per cent of primary schoolchildren and 10 per cent of secondary schoolchildren had been bullied, while 12 per cent of primary school pupils and 6 per cent of those at secondary school were themselves bullies. Children who were bullied were two to three times more likely to have special educational needs.

All but one of the schools continue to be involved in the anti-bullying programmes that the re-searchers have encouraged. They focus on projects in which the children, teachers, supervisors and parents take part.

The measures include encouraging pupils to discuss the subject in class, and to play out roles in the form of drama; providing special training for lunch-time supervisors on how to recognise bullying; improving playgrounds to reduce boredom; giving assertiveness training to timid children and working with bullies to understand the problems of the victims.

In one group of children taking part in the programme there was a 20 per cent reduction in bullying over seven months.

■ Children may have learnt "not to take sweets from strangers" but they are still at risk when they are asked to help, the meeting was told.

Dr David Warden, of the Department of Psychology at Strathclyde University, said that bringing up children to be kind and helpful worked against the "stranger danger" message.

Researchers found that "helpful" children were more likely to comply with a stranger's request for assistance. Simply knowing the "stranger danger" rule was not enough, he said. The message needed to be repeated through primary school life.

One pupil in two says bullying remains a problem, despite efforts to stamp it out

Bullying is still considered to be a big problem by more than half of schoolchildren despite years of official programmes to stamp it out, a survey showed yesterday.

Recent research by ChildLine revealed that 51 per cent of primary pupils and 54 per cent of secondary pupils considered mental and physical abuse by other children to be a menace in their school. Half of primary school pupils and nearly one third of secondary pupils said they had been a victim of bullying during the past term.

The Independent

■ **Author: Celia Hall.**

How to cope with bullying

If you find yourself the victim of group bullying, you must remember that most of the group will simply be following the ring-leader. They will also be frightened of not fitting in, as the bully's attention may turn to them.

What can you do?

Walk away from the situation and then tell someone, i.e. a parent, teacher or Police officer. If you do not feel that you can talk to these people first hand, talk it over with your friends first, see who they suggest. There will always be someone who can help.

Text messages or phone calls - bullying in the 21st century

If you repeatedly receive unpleasant or threatening messages keep a record and tell an adult - even if you know who it is. If it is bullying it needs dealing with.

REMEMBER:-

- Seeming upset will show your aggressors that they're winning.
- Walk tall and be confident.
- Ignore nasty comments and insults.

Bullying can be a terrifying experience. It is vital that you offer to help the victims of bullying.

Here are some examples of behaviour which will help you to decide if someone is being bullied:

- A sudden dislike of certain places or certain journeys i.e. the journey to or from school.
- Suffers from nightmares.
- Becomes withdrawn and anxious.
- School performance starts to suffer.
- Feels ill at certain times every week.
- 'Loses' money and valuable possessions.
- Has unexplained bruises and cuts.
- Cries in secret.

First of all, ask yourself if you could possibly have been involved with the bullying without realising. Have you noticed a person looking uncomfortable when your group of friends have been laughing and joking? If so, put a stop to the bullying immediately by changing the subject of your conversation and letting the victim know that you are on their side.

Bullying

If, as will probably be the case, the bullying is being done by someone else, you have to ask the victim to confide in you. Talk to them sympathetically, explain what cowards the bullies really are and persuade them to talk to someone they trust.

If a victim of bullying does decide to confide in you, it is important that you treat the subject in the correct manner. Here are some pointers:

- Find somewhere quiet to talk.
- Stay calm.
- Take what is said seriously.
- Reassure the victim.
- Build up the victim's confidence so that they can solve their own problems.
- Don't press the victim for information.
- Find out exactly who was involved in the bullying.
- Explain that you are the victim's friend and want to help.
- Try to allay their fears in any way possible.
- If you can't help, find someone who can.

BULLYING CAN DESTROY LIVES. HELP TO STOP IT NOW!

How you can help...

There are many anti-bullying projects that you and your school can get involved with.

Some schools have set up a bullying helpline using teachers or older children as counsellors to help others in the school.

Some schools have set up a bullying court. Teachers and pupils hear cases about real life bullying and decide on what to do with the bully. The bully has to attend and explain why they have behaved in that way. This helps not only the victim, but also the bully.

Youth Action Groups can be very useful to set up anti-bullying projects, or other projects which help to fight crime. To help you with ideas you can speak to your Police Schools Liaison Officer, or ask one of your teachers.
Talk to your teachers and ensure everyone knows the school policy on bullying.

Shoplifting & other forms of theft

Each year businesses lose around £2 billion through shoplifting and other retail crime. Thousands of small items are stolen from businesses each year.

THEY ALL CONTRIBUTE TO THE MASSIVE LOSSES THAT HELP TO PUT COMPANIES OUT OF BUSINESS

Shoplifting isn't just petty crime, it's theft and, as a result, carries a maximum penalty of 7 years imprisonment. It is in all of our interests to deter theft and shoplifting. Just think what would happen if we all helped ourselves to other people's possessions – there would be a complete breakdown of society.

If you have ever stolen or considered stealing from someone else, ask yourself how you would feel if someone decided to help themselves to something of yours. It doesn't matter how small the object is – whether it's a pencil sharpener or £1,000, the crime is still the same: THEFT.

Whether we're involved in shoplifting or not, we all pay the price of the crime through increased costs and poor economic conditions.

Read the following newspaper extract and points of view about shoplifting and theft. Now use your own free choice to decide how serious a crime theft is.

POINTS OF VIEW

- **People work hard for their belongings. No-one else has a right to take them.**
- **Shoplifting is just a nice way of saying theft.**
- **Shoplifting puts companies out of business and people out of work.**
- **We all pay the price of shoplifting through increased costs.**

Young people targeted by criminals

Mobile Phones at risk

Many of you have mobile phones. Mobile phones belonging to young people are one of the hottest targets of street robbery in the UK.

- Make sure you get your phone security marked.
- Keep it out of public view.

Keep your bike safe

Bicycles are popular with thieves - over 100,000 are stolen every year.

- Mark the frame with your postcode and stick on a coded cycle sticker.
- Get a Recorded Cycle form from your local Police station or cycle shop.
- Photograph your bike and record all its details.
- Always lock your bike to something solid like a lamp-post.
- Use a solid metal lock rather than a chain.
- If possible take off your front wheel and lock it to the frame and back wheel.

When you are out and about

Most victims of crime on the streets are young people. Most offenders are also young. Large amounts of cash or property may not be taken but it is very traumatic for the victims.

- Always be aware of where your purse and wallet are.
- Keep any keys in a safe place.
- Keep any valuables such as mobile phones out of sight.
- Leave valuable jewellery at home.

Here is a newspaper extract about Shoplifting. Read it carefully.

Shops count cost of £2bn crime wave

By Dan Conaghan

CRIME is costing shops £2 billion a year, more than a quarter of it as a result of offences by their own staff.

Traders suffered two million crimes last year. Without these offences, profits would have been 25 per cent higher, according to a survey by the British Retail Consortium.

Researchers examined 54,000 shops and stores across Britain with a combined turnover of £62 billion. They found that £560 million was lost as a result of "known criminal activity".

But goods worth more than £1 billion had to be written off as a result and £370 million was spent on security.

"Crime is one of the most serious and costly problems faced by the retail industry in terms of direct losses of product, of the cost of preventative measures and, most worryingly, in the increase of violence and injury to staff," said Mr Keith Ackroyd, BRC chairman.

"Ultimately, it is the consumer and society at large that bears these costs."

He said the survey gave no indication of the physical and emotional effects on shop staff. More than 14,000 were attacked and 106,000 threatened with violence.

There were 178,944 shop burglaries in 1992-93. Ninety five per cent of grocery stores and 90 per cent of electrical, gas and music shops were affected.

Nearly three per cent of these — 17,755 — were ram raids in which vehicles were driven into premises. Burglaries accounted for £331 million, including loss of stock and repair costs.

There were 1,516,481 shoplifting incidents, costing £516·6 million and leading to the arrests of 1·2 million customers and 28,000 staff.

The survey noted that most thefts go unnoticed to be discovered during stocktaking. Retailers often dealt with shoplifting offences themselves rather than call the police.

Mr James May, BRC director general, said: "If every shoplifter was handed over to the police, the whole criminal justice system would grind to a halt."

A spokesman for Marks and Spencer said of the survey: "It will lead to more guards and more sophisticated close circuit television. We have found that shoppers find good security reassuring rather than intimidating and they often tell us they would welcome more."

The survey will be repeated annually by the BRC and will eventually show trends in retail crime. The results will also be incorporated in a database for major retailers who already keep computer records of crime affecting their shops.

- 'Shops count cost of £2bn crime wave' by Dan Conaghan.

DETERRING THEFT CAN OFTEN MEAN TAKING TEMPTATION AWAY FROM THE CRIMINAL

The following pointers will help you and your family to keep your possessions safe and deter crime:

- Always be aware of where your purse or wallet are.
- Store valuables out of sight and in a safe place.
- Always lock your doors.
- Do not reveal your address on luggage labels etc. that are on public view.
- Use timer switches to put lights and TV etc. on when you are out.
- Draw curtains if you go out in the evening.
- Inform Neighbourhood Watch Groups when you go on holiday.
- Cancel milk, bread and paper orders when on holiday.
- Postcode your valuables.
- If your see signs of a break-in at your home, do not go in. Go to a neighbour's and call the Police.

If you know someone who is stealing from another person or shop, it is vital that you try to deter them. You may be afraid to confront them yourself. If so, tell someone you trust, e.g. parents, teachers or youth leaders. They may be able to tackle the problem without telling the culprit who has brought the problem to their attention.

Shoplifting & other forms of theft

What happens if you find yourself caught up in a raid or robbery?

Each situation differs greatly, so the following pointers should be used as guidelines and adapted to suit the situation.

1. If there is a hold-up alarm **ACTIVATE IT** when you feel that it is safe to do so.
2. Always co-operate with the aggressors – if they tell you to lie on the floor, lie on the floor!
3. Avoid sudden and unexpected movements - these could be misinterpreted as escape attempts.
4. Cut your losses:
   - If you are told to fill a bag with money, use the smallest notes first.
   - Stuff the money into a sack. This way less will fit in.
   - Do not draw attention to cash storage points.
5. Watch carefully. Note the criminal's appearance, accent, manner, equipment, methods and getaway vehicles (this will help the Police to track down the robbers).
6. When the robbers have left, **RING THE POLICE IMMEDIATELY.**
   - Ensure that all witnesses stay in the building.
   - Do not discuss what happened with other witnesses, as this could confuse your view of the events.
   - Write down your version of the sequence of events.
   - Do not handle anything that could be used as evidence (fingerprints may have been left behind).

IF YOU ARE OUTSIDE A BUILDING AND SEE A RAID OR ROBBERY TAKING PLACE, DO NOT GET INVOLVED YOURSELF.

CALL THE POLICE IMMEDIATELY.

How you can help...

Theft and shop crime are major concerns for us all. Can you think of any ways of combating these problems in your area? There are a whole range of things that you and your friends can do to reduce the amount of goods stolen from your locality.

HERE ARE SOME IDEAS:

- Set up a cycle / property marking project.
- Do some research into burglaries in your town.
- Make a video about shoplifting and its consequences.
- Produce and circulate a leaflet about crime prevention.
- Find ways of teaching young children the wrongs of stealing.

Again if you set up a Youth Action Group you may be able to combat the problem in your school. Contact your Schools Liaison Officer or your Local Community Safety Officer/Area Constable for help.

Racial Harassment

The term racial harassment refers to any incident which has a racial motive. It includes **personal attacks, written or verbal threats, offensive graffiti or damage to property**. These incidents can happen anywhere - at home, at work, at school or on the streets.

Remember earlier we talked about everyone having a right to feel safe all of the time. This includes feeling free from abuse... there is no reason why any person should be abused because of their race or colour. Imagine how you would feel being picked on because you had blue eyes or black hair. We all have a right to be treated fairly and equally.

Racism doesn't always happen on a large scale; it can take the form of a throwaway comment or remark. A comment which may seem quite innocent to you, may cause a great deal of hurt and upset to someone who is already feeling self-conscious or has suffered racial harassment in the past.

THINK BEFORE YOU SPEAK AND CHALLENGE OTHERS WHO MAKE RACIST REMARKS!

The effects of racial harassment can be absolutely terrifying. Prejudice is something that gets out of hand very easily. Here are some points of view about racial harassment. Read through them carefully to realise just how big a problem racism actually is.

POINTS OF VIEW

- **Racial harassment is something that we must not put up with.**
- **Prejudice is completely unacceptable.**
- **Before you decide to pick on someone because of their colour, ask yourself how you would like to be a victim.**
- **Think before you speak. What may seem like a completely innocent comment to you may upset someone else a great deal.**

HOW YOU CAN HELP...

If you have any ideas for a project that could help to stamp out racial harassment contact your Liaison Officer.

If a victim of racial attack comes to you for help, it is important that you approach the subject sensitively and effectively. The victim will not have chosen you at random and probably believes you to be a person they trust.

Here are some tips:

- If you are the victim of a racial attack or if you witness such an incident, report it to the Police immediately. Remember, the more detail you can give to the Police, the easier it will be for them to identify the culprit and, if necessary, press charges.
- Ensure that you report the incident as a **'racial incident'.**
- Racial incidents may appear to be trivial, but they are very important to the victim.
- The victim should be encouraged to report the incident to the Police or to voluntary organisations.
- No incident is too trivial to report.
- The Police and any other agency will be sympathetic to the victim and will respond positively.

Reproduced by kind permission of The Metropolitan Police

HOW YOU CAN HELP..... **If you have any ideas for a project that could help to stamp out racial harassment in your area, contact your Schools Liaison Officer or your Local Community Safety Officer / Area Constable.**

Power and Control

Harassment can take a number of different forms:

- Verbal or written abuse.
- Abusive behaviour.
- Physical attacks.
- Use and threats of violence.
- Damage to someone's property.
- Intimidation.

Between 2000 and 2001:

- There were 12,455 cases of racial harassment.
- There were 4,257 racially aggravated common assaults.
- There were 4,030 cases of racially aggravated criminal damage.

The worst affected victims were:

- The poorest and families who are unable to move because of cost.
- People who were discriminated against such as ethnic minorities.
- Young people who were not at school or at work.
- Older people and those who are disabled.
- People often have to suffer verbal abuse every day as they go to work or school.

To try and stem this and other problems there are now over 70 Youth Inclusion programmes in place. These are aimed at 13-16 years. The programme offers structured activities and support that will steer this age group away from crime and anti-social behaviour. This programme sets out to:-

- Improve school attendance.
- Reduce school exclusions.
- Prevent youngsters starting on a life of crime.

Research shows that there has been a 30% reduction in arrests following a young person's involvement in the programme. Also there has been a dramatic decrease in crime in areas where these schemes are in operation.

Staying Safe

We would all like to be able to walk through the streets alone without feeling frightened, and we all have a right to be able to feel safe whatever we do. Unfortunately, sometimes that is not always possible so it is important to know what we can do to make sure that we stay safe whatever we do. Most of staying safe is common sense, and although we can't change the actions of others, we can take some steps for ourselves.

We have already talked about the signs that our bodies give us when we feel that something is not right. Once we learn to listen to our bodies, we can recognise dangers early and then we can take the appropriate action. If you start to walk down a dark alley, and your stomach turns and you start sweating because you are nervous, then choose a different route, or find someone to walk with.

ON BUSES AND TRAINS

- Late at night sit downstairs near the driver.
- Don't sit closely to a lone passenger on public transport.
- Do not indicate to others where you will be getting off.

IN TAXIS

- Check that you are using a bona fide company.
- Avoid mini-cabs or private-hire cars that tout for business.
- Always sit behind the driver.

IN THE STREET

- Keep to main, well-lit paths.
- Don't walk closely behind people who are walking alone.
- Don't accept unorganised lifts.
- Invest in a personal alarm.
- Walk facing the traffic.
- If a car stops and you are threatened scream and shout and set off your personal alarm. - **GET AWAY QUICKLY!**
- Think about the clothes you are wearing if you have to walk home late at night, eg. trousers are better than tight skirts.
- If attacked shout **FIRE** – not rape or help, as more people may be likely to respond.
- Carry coins for a phone call.
- Be aware of your surroundings – especially at a cash point, telephone booth, near pubs and clubs.
- Tell someone where you are going and when you will be back.
- Don't carry unreasonable amounts of money.
- Hide valuables, especially mobile phones from view. If you wear a personal stereo remember you can't hear traffic, or someone approaching behind you.
- If you have a bag, keep it closed with the fastening inwards. If you are attacked let the bag go.
- It's best to keep keys in a pocket.
- Especially when in big groups, remember that your shouts and laughter may be seen as threatening to a vulnerable person.

ALONE IN THE HOME

- Don't tell any telephone callers that you are on your own.
- Don't give your name or number when answering the phone.
- Don't have a message on your answerphone that gives your name or number.
- If you receive an abusive or threatening phone-call stay calm and don't say or do anything. Put the receiver down near the phone. Leave it a few minutes and then return and replace it. If it happens again call the operator for advice.
- Ask for the identity card of any officials or people you don't know that call at your house. Always use a door chain.
- Keep samples of identity cards in your home so that you can check their validity.
- If you are worried that an official caller is bogus, ring to check their number or ask them to call back.
- Most identity cards will have a contact number that will allow you to check that your caller is genuine.

WATER SAFETY

- Don't go near water when you're on your own.
- If you fall in, stay calm and try to float on your back.
- If you see someone fall in, **DON'T JUMP IN YOURSELF.** Look for something to pull them out with, i.e. a stick, clothing or a rope. If you can't get them out, throw them a floating object to hold onto then go and get help.
- People can drown in very shallow water. It does not have to be deep to be dangerous.
- When water is frozen, do not walk on it. You do not know how strong the ice is, and if it should break and you fall in, the water will be so cold that you may not be able to get out.
- If you are out walking with a dog and the dog falls into a frozen lake etc., do not follow it in, or you may end up in difficulty yourself. In nearly all recorded accidents the dog has got out on its own accord.
- If you see anyone in difficulty in water, phone the emergency services immediately.

Staying Safe

How you can help

Staying safe doesn't only mean looking after yourself, it means caring for those who can't look after themselves.

Why not do some research to find out which inhabitants need help in your town?

Then you could:

- Keeping children safe is everybody's business. Take notice if you see a young child who seems lost or in distress and do something. Remember they may have been told not to talk to strangers - you may need to get help.
- Provide these people in your area with information about personal safety, security measures, avoiding street crime and bogus callers. This will help to improve understanding between residents of all ages and enable everyone to become more involved in the community.
- Write and perform a home security play for 'vulnerable' residents.
- Offer to help fit door-chains free of charge for elderly people to reduce their fear of crime.
- Make regular visits to elderly and sick people to ensure that they are OK.
- Distribute a specimen identity card list to people who live alone to prevent bogus officials tricking their way into residents' homes.
- Produce a video warning of the dangers of letting strangers into your home.

SAFETY TIPS FOR YOUNG PEOPLE

IF YOU ARE DOING A PART-TIME JOB OR ARE OUT IN THE EVENING

- Be sure your parents know where you are, and how to contact you.
- Go out with friends and return with them.
- If you go out alone, have transport arranged for coming home before you leave.
- If you are out and your lift doesn't turn up, phone and find out why - don't leave alone.
- Don't take a lift with someone you have just met.
- Only take jobs like baby-sitting through friends or family - if you answer an advert take a friend or parent along to check it out.
- If you are baby-sitting get a number where you can call the child's parents.
- Don't open the door to anyone.
- Don't tell anyone who telephones you are on your own.
- On a paper round, never go into a stranger's house or take a lift.
- Wherever you are, make sure you know how to make an emergency phone call and the quickest way out.

STAYING SAFE ON-LINE

- Be careful about people you meet on chat-lines, they may not be what they seem.
- Don't arrange a meeting with someone from a chat-line unless you tell your parents.

Female Safety: A SHARED RESPONSIBILITY

We have already discussed personal safety precautions on the previous page, but here are some extra points that we should consider on the subject of female safety.

Many women are so frightened of being attacked that their quality of life suffers. We must all do whatever we can to reduce their fear.

Here are some suggestions of what men can do to make women feel safer:

- Don't walk behind a woman who is on her own – cross the road.
- Don't sit too close to a single woman on public transport.
- Don't try to be too chatty with a woman who is on her own.
- Remember that your 'friendliness' could be misconstrued as threatening behaviour.
- No staring, whistling, making passing comments - especially if you are in a group of other males.

IF YOU ARE ATTACKED...

It is important that you consider the possibility of attack in advance. Ask yourself if you are physically strong enough to fight back immediately or if you would play along with the attacker and choose your moment to escape.

Whatever you decide, here are some tips that may help you to cope with the experience:

- Move quickly.
- Make as much noise as possible.
- Use your umbrella, hairspray or keys against the attacker.
- Try to breathe deeply and steadily.
- Don't argue.
- Stay as calm as possible.
- Don't fight with the attacker but do try to escape.
- When you do escape, head for a well-lit and populated area.

NOTE: Do NOT be tempted to carry an offensive weapon - a personal alarm would be sensible though.

Self-Defence

One of the best ways of boosting self-confidence and protecting yourself must be the art of self-defence. Naturally, the best way to learn self-defence is through a regular class but, in case you have difficulty getting to a class immediately, here are some self-defence tips.

The art of self-defence is as much about timing as force. You certainly don't have to be the strongest person in the world to practice it, but you do have to be able to target your energies effectively. No matter how frightened you are, it is important that you choose your moment to escape carefully.

- If you are grabbed from the front, bring your hands up through the attacker's arms. Use the heel of your hand to hit his chin or nose.

- A poke in the eye will knock the attacker off balance and often give you enough time to escape. Biting the attacker's hand or arm will also have the same effect.

- If you are grabbed round the neck, take hold of the attacker's little fingers and pull back hard.

- If you see the attacker coming towards you, scream and spit at him. If he manages to take hold of you, knee him in the groin.

- If you are grabbed from behind, stamp on the attacker's foot or scrape your heel down his shin.

If the worst does happen...

If you are attacked, or if someone you know is attacked, **REPORT THE INCIDENT TO THE POLICE IMMEDIATELY.** It could mean the difference between an arrest and the attacker striking again.

Do not be afraid to report the incident. Your case will be treated sympathetically and in confidence. Police forces have specially-trained officers who will be able to give you the advice and counselling you need. Remember to that it is a serious crime whether it is committed by a stranger or someone you know.

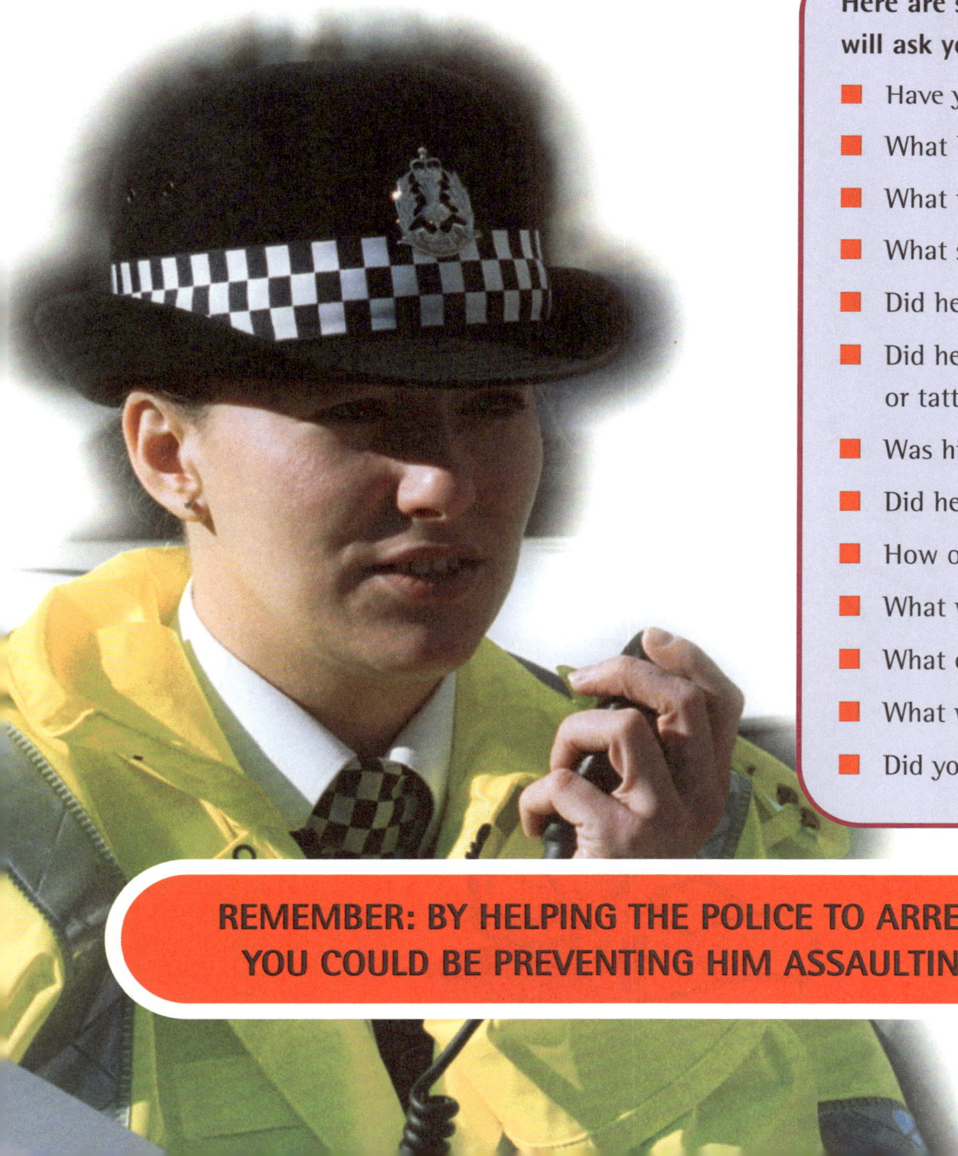

Whilst you are waiting to speak to the Police:

- Write down all the facts that you can remember about the attack.
- Do not drink alcohol.
- **DO NOT WASH OR CHANGE YOUR CLOTHES.**

The Police will want to know as many details as possible about your attacker.

Here are some things that the Police will ask you about:

- Have you seen the man before?
- What height / build was he?
- What was his hair like?
- What shape was his face?
- Did he have a moustache or beard?
- Did he have any distinguishing marks or tattoos?
- Was his mouth wide or narrow?
- Did he have an accent?
- How old was he?
- What was his complexion like?
- What colour were his eyes?
- What was he wearing?
- Did you see which way he went?

REMEMBER: BY HELPING THE POLICE TO ARREST YOUR ATTACKER YOU COULD BE PREVENTING HIM ASSAULTING SOMEONE ELSE

How can you help?

Here are some ideas for projects on female safety:

- Carry out a community crime survey.
- Interview young women in your area and collect their thoughts on crime.
- Distribute information about staying safe.
- Distribute information about personal alarms.
- Provide advice on self-defence.
- Organise an Activity Safety Day for young women.
- Hold discussions with local councillors and other community leaders to bring about improvements in street-lighting conditions etc.
- Organise personal safety displays at local shows, fêtes etc.

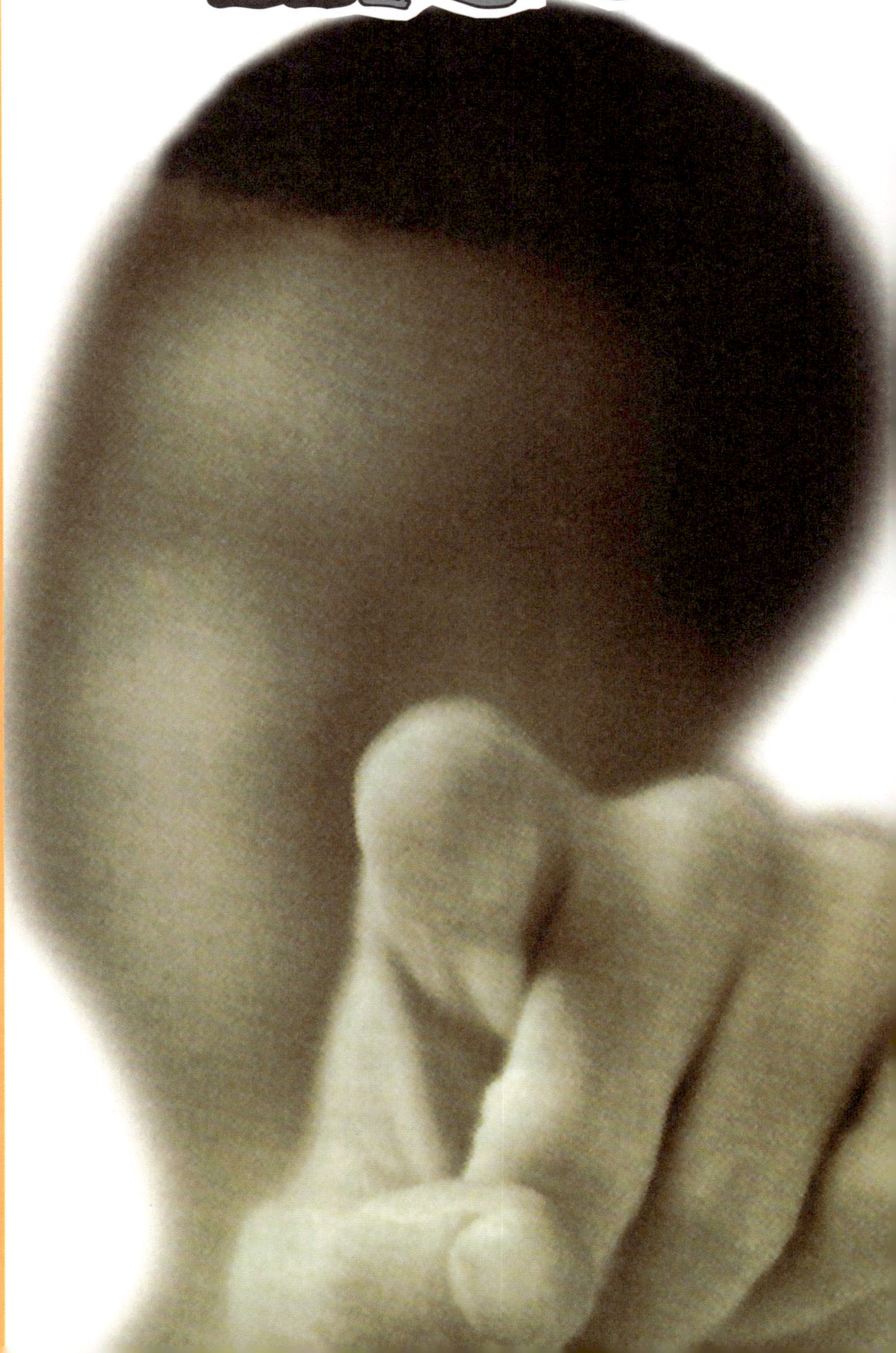

Trespass and Vandalism

What is Trespass?

Trespass is interfering with another person's property or unlawfully entering their land. This law does not exist in this form in Scotland.

What is Vandalism?

Vandalism is the act of damaging property, destroying what is beautiful or interfering with things that are not meant to be touched by the public.

The effects

The world may be an exciting place, but it is also a very dangerous one. A great many people are injured and killed every year through the irresponsible and destructive behaviour of vandals. It is important to remember that laws and regulations exist to protect us from danger. This is also true of safety fences and walls. By breaking laws, regulations or safety provisions, we are putting ourselves and others at risk.

Before we look at the various types of trespass and vandalism, it is important that we appreciate just how serious the implications are. Read the following newspaper extract, then ask yourself if trespass and vandalism are acceptable forms of behaviour.

■ **VANDALISM – damaging or destroying property**

HERE IS A NEWSPAPER EXTRACT ABOUT VANDALISM. READ IT CAREFULLY.

School vandals run up £8m bill

VANDALS and fire-raisers caused more than £8m damage to Scottish schools last year, a watchdog body has revealed.

Audit Scotland pointed out that as well the financial impact, the anti-social behaviour also lowered morale and led to lost teaching time. It accused some councils of failing to make "sufficient progress" in tackling the problem.

Its report showed nine out of the 32 councils took the brunt of the problem, suffering 70% of the total recorded costs. It also indicated that vandalism alone cost some councils almost £6000 per school in 1999-2000.

Glasgow City Council was the worst affected by vandalism, having to pay out £1,327,100, a cost of £17 per pupil. However it, along with South Lanarkshire, East Dunbartonshire and Dundee City, was applauded by Audit Scotland for making good progress "in the face of medium to high levels of vandalism", but Aberdeenshire, Fife and North Ayrshire were criticised.

A Glasgow City Council spokesman said: "We are obviously pleased our efforts have been recognised because we work extremely hard in tackling school vandalism in various ways. We have improved security measures in and around buildings and we also run a major staff development programme on school security."

Schools were being encouraged to identify security problems and possible solutions themselves. The spokesman also said there were plans for 29 secondary schools to have the latest security and anti-vandalism measures.

Fife Council admitted that, despite more than 300 CCTV cameras in schools, more needed to be done to deter vandals.

Councillor Kay Morrison, education vice-chair, said they had invested more than £2m in school security since 1997 and some measures had started to produce a reduction in vandalism in key areas.

"However, we still face a significant annual bill as a result of mindless vandalism and this is not acceptable.

"In schools that have experienced spates of intense vandalism it is often the pupils and teachers who suffer the most as countless boarded windows undoubtedly have an effect on morale. We must strive to protect them by providing a safe and welcoming teaching environment."

The report revealed the bill for this property crime last year was £100,000 higher than the previous 12 months, although down on the £12m total in 1994-95.

Researchers found 65% of headteachers believe the problem of vandalism either has remained the same or worsened in the last few years.

They also discovered school fires caused £2.6m of damage, although Strathclyde and Lothian and Borders fire brigades both reported drops.

The findings follow a series of recommendations to councils by Audit Scotland four years ago on tackling property crime in schools.

The latest report, A Safer Place Revisited, was designed to provide an update on the progress made by councils since then. It maintained many schools still suffered from high levels of vandalism and fire which not only had a financial cost but lowered morale and affected teaching time.

While some councils were doing particularly well, progress in others had been mixed. It said the three identified needed to do a lot more.

Audit Scotland concluded that councils which had not implemented all its recommendations should make a greater commitment to tackle the problem. It suggested they collect information on where and when vandalism and fire-raising happen and target those schools as a priority.

It also urged local authorities to work closely with the school and local community in developing appropriate measures while monitoring the situation.

Reacting to the report, the Convention of Scottish Local Authorities said the "determined efforts" of councils to tackle fire and vandalism had been acknowledged. Councillor Danny McCafferty, Cosla's education and children's issues spokesman, said he was pleased the sustained effort by local authorities had seen the costs incurred by fire and vandalism reduced by a third in a relatively short period of time.

"However, further improvements can be made and councils are not complacent about the problem by any means. Councils recognise that property crime is still a major problem."

Author: Raymond Duncan

Reproduced by kind permission of The Herald

Major Targets

Vandalism of telephone boxes

At least 1,000 telephone boxes are vandalised or attacked **every week.** Many of the attacks result from boredom, but their consequences can be far more serious.

Public telephones can be vital lifelines, not only for those who do not have a telephone of their own, but for anyone who finds themselves involved in an accident or emergency situation.

Remember that to damage a public telephone may mean that you are preventing someone from making a life saving call to the emergency services. Your actions could cost lives. If you know someone who has vandalised a public phone box, explain to them that they might be preventing someone from making a life saving call to the emergency services. **Their actions could cost lives.**

Railway trespass and vandalism

Millions of people use public transport every day. We must all act responsibly to ensure their safety. Railways are extremely dangerous places. During 2001, 307 people were killed on railways and 2,672 people suffered injuries.

It is vital that you stay well away from railway lines and never damage the surrounding fences. Overhead wires and fittings on the railway carry 25,000 volts of electricity, these can kill you even if you don't touch them, electricity can jump several feet.

Express trains travel at speeds of up to 140 mph and high speed trains can take up to **one and a half miles to stop.** By standing close to these trains you run a serious risk of being sucked under.

Don't leave anything on railway lines or throw objects at trains. **Remember trains run on tracks and cannot swerve to avoid obstructions.** Obstructing a railway line is not only irresponsible, but also a very serious criminal offence.

Major Targets

Graffiti

You may think that graffiti is just a minor offence. Yet stop to think what image it portrays.

Graffiti is a sign of an unsafe, unfriendly area. As the appearance of a town deteriorates, the inhabitants stop caring and crime takes hold. We need to improve our area, not turn it into a no-go area. By stamping out graffiti, we could invest the thousands of pounds which are usually used to clean it up in improved local facilities.

Besides undermining the environment, vandals often endanger themselves in an attempt to get their graffiti in the most prominent position. Accident and Emergency Departments treat the many serious injuries suffered by vandals who have fallen from high buildings and motorway bridges.

If you know someone who is vandalising property with graffiti, talk to them about the problem. Suggest that they use their energies on something more constructive. Many of these people are talented artists. Persuade them to use their talents for the good of the community.

Motorway trespass and vandalism

Motorways are designed for drivers, not pedestrians. There can be few places more dangerous for a young person to trespass. With cars travelling at speeds in excess of 70 mph there is little chance that a person walking on the carriageway would survive.

Although few young people are silly enough to wander onto the motorway, some amuse themselves by throwing objects at cars from motorway bridges.

SUCH ACTIONS ARE VERY DANGEROUS AND CAUSE SERIOUS INJURY AND DEATH.

Think before you act...
If you know someone who is trespassing on a motorway or damaging property, inform the Police IMMEDIATELY!

Litter

Dumping litter is another form of vandalism. Discarded carrier bags, household waste and rubbish can kill animals and small children. Glass, tins and hypodermic needles pose obvious threats, but even piles of seemingly harmless wrappers and newspapers are dangerous. It was this kind of waste which fuelled the fires that killed 56 people at Bradford City Football Ground and 31 at Kings Cross Station.

You may think that you are doing no harm by throwing away one sweet wrapper, but consider what would happen if everyone in the UK did the same – 56 million wrappers would no longer be such a minor problem!

Although we rarely hear of people being fined for dropping the odd piece of litter, there is a maximum penalty of £1,000 for the offence. It's up to us all to keep our streets clean. If you know someone who is dumping litter, explain to them what a serious problem they are causing and help to put a stop to our litter problem.

VANDALISM AND TRESPASS ARE DIFFICULT TO COMBAT ALONE. IF YOU HAVE ANY INFORMATION ON THESE CRIMES, PLEASE CONTACT THE POLICE IMMEDIATELY.

How can you help?

Vandalism is something that we should all take very seriously. Can you think of ways to combat it? Here are some ideas:

- Write and circulate an anti-vandalism newsletter to local households.
- Suggest that your school, community centre etc. purchase some anti-vandalism paint.
- Organise an anti-vandalism poster competition.
- Erect anti-vandalism signs.
- Make a video about vandalism and its consequences.
- Write and perform an anti-vandalism play.
- Meet members of the local council to see if they can organise the painting of a mural on a youth centre wall. Encourage youngsters to use the wall instead of spreading graffiti across the town.

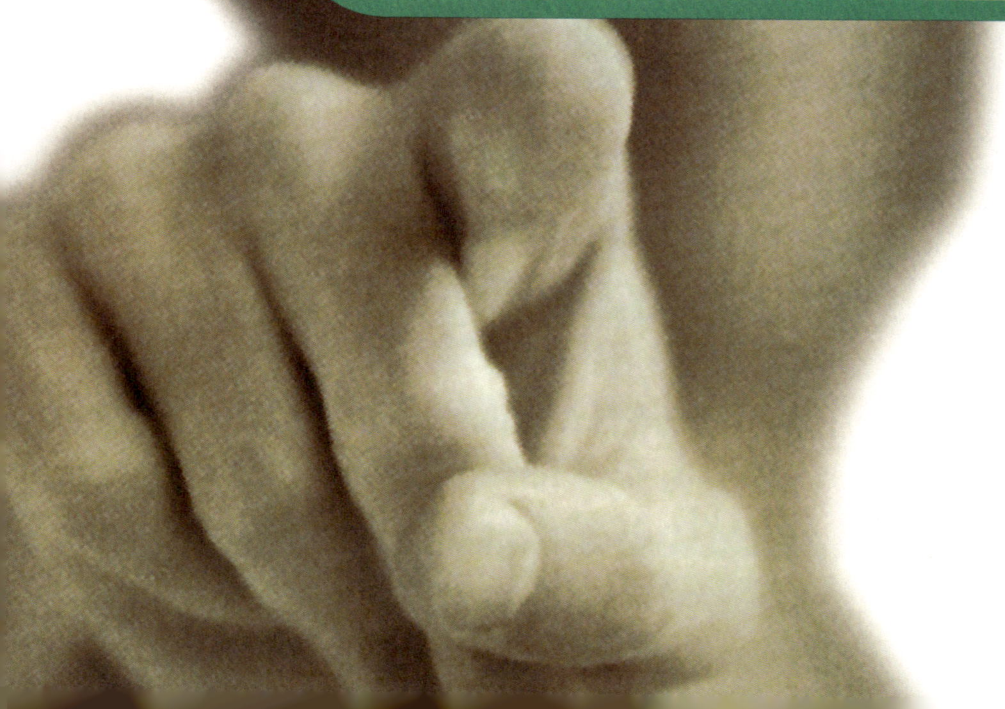

Crime Prevention Panels

Now that you're switched on to existing methods of crime prevention and avoidance, you're probably brimming with ideas of your own. If so, you could be just the kind of person we're looking for to set up a crime prevention panel.

Crime Prevention Panels are groups of local people who meet on a regular basis to combat crime. They work with the Police and other citizens' organisations to make their environment a safer place to live.

Panel members should have a sound knowledge of their area and its problems. They must be enthusiastic, determined and dedicated to making a real difference to their community. Because the panels are made up of local residents, they can make a real difference to people's lives without causing resentment.

The aims of Crime Prevention Panels are to:

- Reduce opportunities for crime.
- Help and reassure those who live in fear of crime.
- Develop closer communities.
- Design interesting and absorbing activities for young people to prevent them drifting into crime.

During the course of their work, the panels split up into teams to focus on specific problems. They research their area of concern and introduce Crimebeat-style projects to combat targeted problems.

Most areas have an existing crime prevention panel. If you contact your local panel, they could help you to set up a youth panel in your school. Alternatively, they may be considering having a representative from a school on their panel. Either way, it is a great opportunity for you and your school to get involved with the local community and help to fight crime.

It is vital that people of your age play an active part in crime prevention. You are in an ideal position to influence your peers and can use your own personal experience and knowledge to prevent other youngsters getting involved in crime.

If you think you've got what it takes to get involved with a Crime Prevention Panel, contact your local Police station for information on what action you can take.

What's in it for me?

Working alongside the Police or in community groups can be fun. Activities vary across the country. Often there are challenging projects aimed at reducing crime that give people the chance to win prizes and trophies.

Being a good citizen can mean a national award for you or your group. There are the Phillip Lawrence Awards which are open for young people aged 11-20. These recognise outstanding achievements in good citizenship by young people. They are awarded annually by the National Youth Agency.

Speak to your Local Community Safety Officer to see if any of the following examples are available in your area.

- A competition which involves the Police and the other emergency services.
- Community musical events with inputs from young DJ's and groups.
- The chance of a place on a driving course for older teenagers.

Anti-Social Behaviour

What's it all about?

Anti-social behaviour is something that disturbs others and destroys the peace and quiet of a neighbourhood.

It can be caused by a noisy party, groups of people shouting or graffiti. Even pets and animals can cause a nuisance continually barking or running around into neighbours' gardens, parks and playgrounds.

'Young people and students are most likely to tell others that they have suffered from anti-social behaviour.'

Neighbours from hell

When the new neighbours moved in we were really pleased, but this was not to last. After a few days they started playing their radios and stereos really loud late at night. Their dog started coming into our garden through a hole in the fence and making a mess all over the lawn.

My mum went round to complain but they just shouted at her and slammed the door in her face. The last straw was on Saturday night when they had a party which went on until 5 am in the morning together with their car alarm going off throughout the night.

My dad said he's going to get the Environmental Health Department or the Police to come round and speak to them.

What a noise!

Noise can be a big problem. People may play their radios too loud, hold parties late into the night and use their vacuum cleaners into the early hours. They may also leave their car alarms going all night. Noise can be worse on estates, in blocks of flats, and where people live close together.

Remember if you go and talk to the person about the level of noise

- Stay calm and quietly spoken
- Listen to the other person's point of view
- Don't shout at them. Stay in control
- Explain the problem
- Don't interrupt the other person when they are speaking
- If they cannot be reasoned with, calmly leave and inform the local Environmental Health Department or the Police.

Noise Problems

Noise problems can include:

- Barking dogs.
- DIY activities.
- Loud stereos.
- Screaming and shouting.
- Banging doors.
- Noisy parties.
- Alarms going off all night.
- Verbal and physical abuse.

What can you do?

- Speak to them.
- Tell the Environmental Health Agencies.
- Report them to the RSPCA.
- Tell the Police.
- Ring the Local Housing Services..

Vehicle Noise

Vehicle noise can be caused by both adults and young people. It can lead to arguments and even fights. Remember if you talk to someone about the problem remain calm.

- Banging doors late at night.
- Playing car stereos and radios very loudly.
- Carrying out noisy repairs in driveways late at night.

If there is a real problem report it to the Environmental Health Services, in extreme circumstances report it to the POLICE. If there is an emergency then dial 999.

Fly Tipping

Anti-social behaviour creates an environment in which more serious crime can take hold.

It can occur anywhere:

- In people's homes and gardens.
- On estates.
- In town centres.
- Shopping parades.
- In urban and rural area.

It blights people's lives, undermines the fabric of society and holds back regeneration'...
White Paper Respect and Responsibility.

It is not right for people to:

- Store lots of rubbish in their gardens.
- Fly tip (This is when rubbish is dumped in streams, over walls or on lay-bys, anywhere that people can rid of it).
- Dump rubbish out in the country.

Storing rubbish can encourage vermin such as rats, mice and other creatures. It is also a breeding ground for flies and germs. Basically it is very anti-social to store rubbish in your garden. It is a health risk and it can be dangerous.

Fly tipping is something which is to be discouraged. Taking your rubbish and dumping it somewhere else is 'not on'. Other people then have to deal with it. Animals may be killed, people may be injured and it can be very dangerous to just leave rubbish on the side of the road. If you see someone doing this, take their number and tell the Police.

Dumping rubbish out in the country can be dangerous. It is a fire hazard, it can injure farm animals. Liquids may also leak out and get into the soil and crops.

The environment and health services need to be contacted if you think there is a build up of rubbish and a danger to health. There may be fumes or gases coming from it or it might just smell really awful. If there is unaccounted rubbish anywhere in your area report it to the local Environmental and Health Unit at your council. If you feel it is dangerous then ring the Police.

REMEMBER...
IF THERE IS ENOUGH EVIDENCE AND THE PEOPLE THAT CAUSED THE TROUBLE DO NOTHING AFTER A WARNING, ENVIRONMENTAL AND HEALTH WILL TAKE THE MATTER FURTHER.

Drugs and Alcohol

'Anti-social behaviour means different things to different people.'

For example:-

- Crack houses run by drugs dealers.
- Drunken 'yobs' in the town centre.
- Drug addicts in communal areas.

When there are drug users or alcoholics in the area there may be a lot of noise, fights, disturbances and verbal abuse. If houses or flats are being used for dealing then they may be very busy causing lots of noise and disturbance.

Drugs and alcohol lead to crime, as the users need to get funds. Muggings go up, theft and burglaries increase. Often offenders are teenagers.

What can you do?

- Work as a community against it.
- Make sure that you stay away from these areas if you can.
- Inform the authorities if things get out of hand.

Ways in which areas are dealing with the problem:

- Local child curfew schemes. These have been enforced for children up to 15 years of age.
- anti-social behaviour orders to deal with serious but not necessarily criminal behaviour by those aged 10 and above.
- Powers to remove truants to certain buildings to allow the Police, schools and local authorities to work with these youngsters.
- Final warning scheme. To replace Police cautions of young people.
- Parenting orders to help reinforce and support the responsibility of parents.

If there was a lot of drug taking or people drinking alcohol in your area what would you do?

What a mess!

What would you have done?

It was late one Saturday afternoon, dad and mum were in the living room watching the television. Joe and his sister were outside playing football. All was quiet next door.

Joe enjoyed passing the ball whilst his sister Megan liked heading the ball back to him. Joe passed the ball to Megan who went to head the ball back. Unfortunately she missed it. The ball bounced once and then disappeared into next door's garden.

Joe climbed over the fence to get the ball. Once on the other side he eventually spotted it on the other side of an abandoned car which was overgrown with weeds. He climbed onto the car so that he could reach for the ball.

Next door's garden was a real mess. There was the abandoned car and then an old wardrobe which had the doors falling off it. There was a broken down dog kennel in the corner and lots of old cans and tins which seemed to be half full of an assortment of liquids.

As Joe leant across the bonnet of the rusty car he slipped and fell between the wing and the half opened door. He tumbled to the ground and felt the warm trickle of blood down his sleeve. He lay on the ground, heard a noise above him and saw to his horror the wreck of the car move slightly and then topple over trapping him underneath. He cried out for his sister. She looked over the fence, saw what had happened and rushed into the house for help....

Our Estate

Look at this plan. You will see some areas have been highlighted in red and some in green. The red areas are those where there might be problems. The green areas are the safest.

Red areas could include places where drug addicts hang out, where there are crack houses or walls that vandals pick for spraying graffiti.

Make a plan of your area. Which parts are the safest and which do you think are the most dangerous? Use the same colour code as the map above.

What kind of problems do you have where you live?

Taking things further

If there has been a problem and you need to take further action this is what might happen.

- Formal warning to individuals.
- Warning in writing to the individuals and parents.
- Review of what has happened so far and thoughts about what can be done in the future.
- Once an ASBO (anti-social behaviour order) is asked for there will be regular contact between the different people.
- Once things have been decided an ASBO is issued at once.
- A report appears in the press.
- A leaflet is produced for the people living in the area.

Legal Action

If the problem with noise or trouble becomes serious and is not solved then legal action may be taken.

Criminal proceeding

If a crime has been committed the Police may charge someone and take them to court. They could be fined, put on probation or have to take part in community service. In a serious case they may even go to prison.

Possession

The council can, if the rules have been broken and things get really bad, threaten to take someone's home away from them. This is often enough to stop someone from being a nuisance.

Injunction

This comes from the court and either stops someone from doing something or makes them do something. It is normally used if violence is possible or if violence has been used. They can also be used for noise. If it is broken people could be fined or sent to prison.

Anti-Social Behaviour Order

It can be used in anti-social behaviour. It can stop someone being anti-social or keep them out of a certain area. It usually lasts for at least two years.

Of just over 118,000 neighbour noise incidents reported, almost half of those substantiated were resolved informally. Of the remainder, where formal steps were taken, only a few hundred ended up in Court but over 80% of those summoned were convicted and noise equipment - stereos and TVs - were seized on more than 200 occasions.

A Personal Story...

'I was fed up with school. It was just so boring. I never seemed to be any good at anything and the others in my class always got more marks than I did. That was when I started 'bunking off.'

It began with one afternoon a week, but as time went on it increased to twice or three times every week. It was dead easy as I used to write my own notes and then give them to the teacher the following day.

Instead of going to school I would go down to the arcade in the high street for a couple of hours. It was here that I meet Jeff who introduced me to the gang on the estate.

Most days I would go down to the estate with the gang. We would then hang around the garages or the play areas. We used to shout abuse at the old people as they walked across the park or we might go and taunt the young mothers who went to the swings with their children. But it didn't stop there, we liked making a noise as well and used to play our stereos really loud. Then if we were really bored we would go and cause trouble in one of the local shops or mess about with an abandoned car.

People used to say we were being anti-social but we didn't know what that meant and we didn't care.

That's all stopped now. I was caught by the Police spraying graffiti on a wall and also stealing from a local shop. I was sent back to school and my parents got into serious trouble.

I have now joined a Youth Inclusion Programme which is run locally. A lot of my mates belong. We do all sorts of things on this programme and have a great time. I haven't been in trouble for several months now and people say I am a changed person.'

Domestic Violence

Domestic violence can be

- PHYSICAL
- FINANCIAL
- EMOTIONAL
- SEXUAL

...abuse within the home.

90% OF ALL REPORTED CASES ARE BY MEN ON WOMEN

Domestic violence can involve:

- Slapping.
- Hitting.
- Punching.
- Bruising.
- Holding.

Here are some other things that might happen:

- Choking.
- Pulling hair.
- Burning.
- Using weapons.
- Pinning someone against the wall.
- Making threats.
- Calling someone names.
- Leaving obscene messages.
- Humiliating someone.......

the list goes on and on......

- **One in 4 women suffer from domestic violence in their lives.**
- Around 3.6 million people are told every year by others that they have suffered from domestic violence.
- 50% of those experiencing domestic violence have children under 16 in their homes.

When Sam arrived at the refuge she was quite badly bruised and had cuts on her arms. She told the others how her partner had hit her again and again when he got angry. She was pushed down the stairs and one time she was hit with a chair. Her two children aged 10 and 14 years had experienced the violence themselves when he had turned on them after they had helped their mother clean up after one of their arguments.

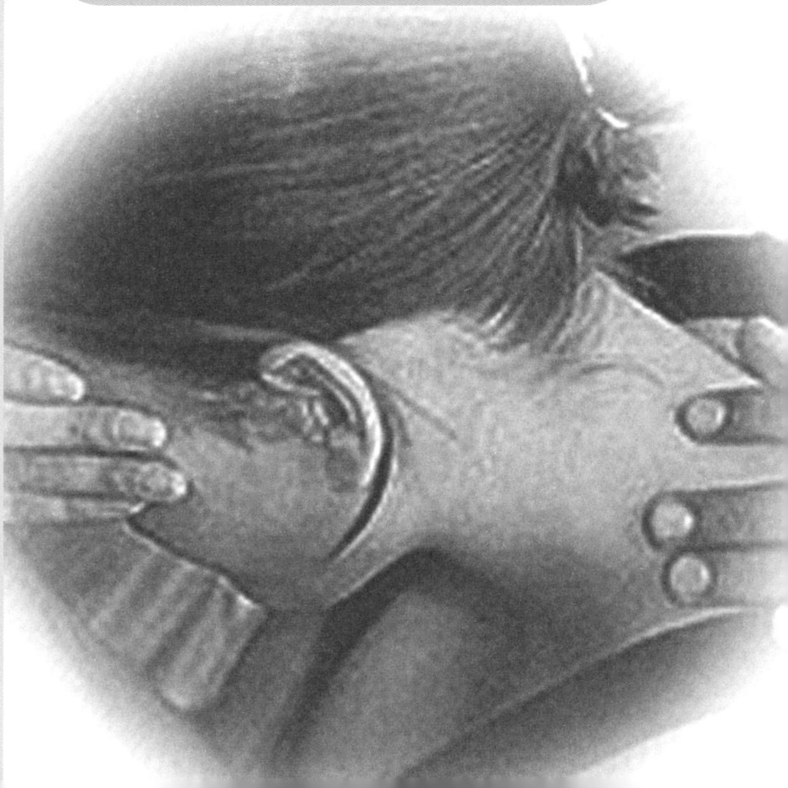

Some facts and consequences

Fact

- People are often affected by domestic violence years later.
- Parents can use violent language against their children.
- Parents can find it difficult to protect their children.

Consequence

- Individuals may be unable to carry out ordinary tasks.
- Children can be left confused about what is going on.
- Children may lack respect for the non-abuser.
- Children could suffer at school.
- Children may find they don't want to go to school but stay at home instead to protect an abused member of the family.

In addition those suffering may...

- Not be allowed to use the phone.
- Be forced to move to a remote area.
- Not be allowed to leave the house on their own.
- Be isolated from friends and family.
- In very extreme cases be denied warmth, food, toilet or washing facilities.

After suffering like this those who have been abused feel unwanted and lack confidence.

What could they do?

Ricky's Story...

Ricky had watched whilst his father had hit his mother several times. Once when he was in bed he heard them fighting and crept out onto the landing and saw his father hit his mother with a hairbrush. Ricky never told anyone what had happened. When he was about 18 years old he had a real problem with his relationship with girls and it was a long time before he went out on his first date. Ricky often had nightmares remembering the way his father had treated his mother.

Chloe's Story...

Chloe had spent her childhood in a flat in an inner city estate. Her father had come and gone. Often he would spend days away from home. When he came back to visit he would only give her mother a few pounds. He always took away any credit cards and if he thought she had spent anything he would lock her in the bedroom for hours. Chloe often went without food, and sometimes they would only have one meal a day. Chloe's life was very hard and she would often spend nights huddled under a blanket, as they could not afford to have any heat on. Her mother never forgave her father for what he had done to her and Chloe.

What do you think they should have done?

Personal Safety Plan

When young people are attacked at home or see one of their parents attacked it usually has a dramatic effect on them.

They may...

- Feel fear, anger and shame.
- Seem to be powerless to change things.
- Cannot concentrate.
- Be confused.
- Find it difficult to sleep and eat.
- Be nervous and tense.
- Get frightened easily.
- Become quiet and withdrawn.

Children who suffer from domestic violence may...

- Find it difficult to mix with others.
- Become aggressive.
- Seek attention.
- Find it difficult to communicate with others.
- Have problems making friends.
- May wet the bed or suffer from stomach aches or sickness.

If you suffer from any form of domestic violence it is important that you have your own **Personal Safety Plan (PSP)**:

Whilst under attack

- Look for a way out.
- Practice getting out of your home safely.
- Have a bag packed.
- Have a code word that means ring for help.
- Work out where you will go if you are attacked.

After an attack

- Call the Police.
- Go to a solicitor if you can.
- Tell a teacher, friend or someone you trust.

Remember to make your home safe

Safe Home

- Buy and fit new locks if you are allowed.
- Make sure that everyone suffering knows about the PSP.
- Make sure schools and play centres know who can pick up the children.
- Tell your neighbours that if they see the abuser nearby they should call the Police.

Forms of Abuse

We tend to think of abuse as physical violence or assault. In reality abuse is the summary of physical, sexual and physological abusive behaviours directed by one person to another. Abusers often use these behaviours to control other people and get their way.

Financial Abuse

Money and responsibility become tools by which the abuser can further control the victim, it can include the following:

- preventing them from getting or keeping a job
- having to account for every penny they spend
- demanding their money
- forcing them to beg or commit crimes for money

Marion's Story...

Marion found it difficult to make ends meet. Gary always demanded her pay packet at the end of the week and then went out and spent it all on drink and gambling. He did not allow her to have a credit card or cheque book.

Physical Abuse

Physical assault is the most obvious form of domestic violence, the most visible and ultimately the most lethal.

Physical abuse is any act of violence on a victim.

- slapping
- kicking
- shoving
- choking
- pinching
- forced feeding
- pulling hair
- punching
- throwing things
- burning
- beating
- use of objects
- physical restraint - pinning against a wall, floor, bed etc.

Emotional Abuse

Many forms of abuse are cruel. Emotional abuse is more subtle. Quite often such abuse goes unseen, as even the victim does not recognise that they are being abused. Although emotional abuse does not leave physical marks, it is often more seriously damaging to their self esteem. Emotional abuse often follows physical or sexual abuse.

Isolation

- checking up on you
- moving to an isolated area
- ensuring you lack transport or a telephone
- making your friends feel uncomfortable when they visit so they stop coming
- demanding a report on your actions and conversations
- not allowing any activity which excludes the abuser
- finding fault with your friends/family

Verbal Abuse

- yelling or shouting at you
- making threats
- insulting you
- being sarcastic or critical of your interests, opinions or beliefs
- humiliating you in private or in company
- refusing to discuss issues which are important to you
- laughing or making fun of you
- leaving nasty messages

Sexual Abuse

Few crimes affect victims as severely as those of sexual abuse.

Definitions of Sexual Abuse

The involvement of children under the age of 17 in sexual activities with any person having care, custody or control of them; activities which they do not truly understand or to which they are unable to give informed consent, or that cross the boundaries of normal family roles.

(Schechtor and Roberge)

Sexual abuse involves forcing or pressurising a young person to take part in sexual activities, whether or not the child is aware of what is happening.

The activities might involve physical contact such as intimate touching, fondling and cuddling, or even penetration (rape). It can also include non-contact activities such as being forced to look at pornographical material, watch sexual activity, pose for photographs or videos in sexual ways or being encouraged to behave in any sexually inappropriate ways.

(Working Together to Safeguard Children)

Both men and women can be abusers and the abuse often occurs when a trusting relationship has been established between the abuser and their victim. e.g. with a parent, grandparent, family friend, babysitter, neighbour.

Unfortunately sexual abuse is still very much a taboo subject within our society, despite the fact that it can involve people of every race, gender, age and class. If a young person is being sexually abused it is unlikely that they will talk openly about it and each individual victim can react very differently. Often there are no physical scars or bruises, but more often behavioural changes. Specific effects can depend on the time period over which the abuse has occurred, the relationship between the abuser and the abused and the character of the victim themselves.

Common Reactions...

shock — feeling dirty — fear of not being believed

guilt — anger — hopelessness — shame

feeling contaminated — panic attacks — severe signs of distress

tendency to silence — withdrawal — powerlessness — sleeping problems

eating disorders — phobias — bed-wetting — hints about sexual activity

fear of being morally judged — fear of being blamed for the abuse

flashbacks — not wanting to be left alone with someone — violent behaviour

self-destructive behaviour — lack of self-esteem — confusion

changes in performance at school — inability to make friends

HOW YOU CAN HELP

DON'T...

- Overwhelm the victim with your own feelings
- Interrupt
- Pry or question
- Make promises you can't keep

DO...

- Take them seriously
- Stay calm
- Comfort them
- Listen very carefully
- Give time and patience
- Develop trust
- Praise their courage
- Reassure them
- Tell them they are not responsible
- Make them feel secure

EVERY YOUNG PERSON HAS THE RIGHT TO BE PROTECTED FROM SEXUAL ABUSE

A Personal Story...

Even though a victim of sexual abuse will want the abuse to stop, they may still love the abuser and they may be frightened about getting them into trouble.

If the abuse is going to be stopped for good, the local Child Protection Unit, Social Services and the Police may all be called on for help and advice, but the victim should not be pressurised into making a complaint. It is important to make sure that the victim knows that officials from such organisations are their friend and not their enemy. The abuser might well have told the victim that the police etc are 'out to get them'.

Lisa's Story...

Lisa was 5 years old when her grandad started abusing her. She would go to stay overnight with him and her grandma sometimes when her mum had to work night shifts. At first grandad said it was a special game just between the two of them, but over time he became more and more forceful, coming to her room at night and ignoring her when she said she was frightened and uncomfortable and asked him to stop. She knew what her grandad did to her was wrong and also felt that her grandma really knew what was going on, but didn't say or do anything to make it stop. Her grandad had also warned Lisa that if she told anyone about their 'special secret' he would tell Lisa's mum that she had asked him to do these things to her and make her mum send her away.

It was only when Lisa was 15 years old and her grandad had died that she felt she could speak out about what had happened to her all those years ago. She had always found it difficult to make friends, her self-esteem was very low and she suffered feelings of acute anxiety, agitation and guilt, still partly believing what her grandad had told her, that she was to blame for the way he behaved.

Lisa's only wish is that she knew then what she knows now...

THERE ARE PEOPLE AND SERVICES WHO CAN AND WANT TO HELP!

Help is at Hand

A number of agencies are working to combat the problems of anti-social behaviour

POLICE

- They are able to apply for anti-social behaviour orders.
- Pick up children who should be at school.
- Work on Police community projects.
- Reassure the public.

SCHOOLS and LOCAL EDUCATION AUTHORITIES

- They can prepare special work for truants.
- Work with the Police and other agencies.
- Target work at adults with poor basic skills and the unemployed.
- Work with the community.

ENVIRONMENTAL SERVICES

- Quickly remove abandoned vehicles.
- Remove graffiti.
- Keep the streets clean.
- Control noise.
- Improve open spaces and lighting in the area.

FIRE and RESCUE SERVICES

- Respond to arson incidents.
- Remove vehicles thought to be a fire risk.
- Investigate hoax calls and arson attacks.

YOUTH OFFENDING TEAMS

- Work with young offenders and those at risk of offending.
- Spot problems at an early stage.

NEIGHBOURHOOD WATCH

- Mark property.
- Gather intelligence.
- Raise awareness.

LOCAL NEWSPAPERS, RADIO AND TELEVISION

- Raise awareness.
- Name and shame.
- Provide positive stories.

If you need help...

GENERAL

AGE CONCERN Tel: 0800 009966

ANTI-BULLYING CAMPAIGN Tel: 0207 378 1446

ASSOCIATION OF BRITISH INSURERS (ABI)
Tel: 020 7 600 3333
Website: http://www.abi.org.uk

BRAKE Tel: 01484 559 909
Website: http://www.brake.org.uk

BRITISH TRANSPORT POLICE
Tel: 0207 828 1212

CHARTERED INSTITUTE OF ENVIRONMENTAL HEALTH Tel: 0207 928 6006
Website: http://www.cieh.org.uk

CHILDLINE Tel: 0800 1111 (Ireland: 1 800 666 666)
Website: http://www.childline.org.uk

COMMISSION FOR RACIAL EQUALITY
Tel: 0207 828 7022
Website: http://www.cre.gov.uk

CRIME CONCERN TRUST Tel: 01793 863 500
Website: http://www.crimeconcern.org.uk

CRIMESTOPPERS Tel: 0800 555 111
Website: http://www.crimestoppers-uk.org

CRIMINAL INJURIES COMPENSATION AUTHORITY Tel: 0207 8426800

DEPT. TRANSPORT, ENVIRONMENT & REGIONS
Tel: 020 7944 3000

ENCAMS Tel: 02890 471144
Website: http://www.encams.org

HOME OFFICE Tel: 020 7 273 3963

HOME OFFICE CRIME REDUCTION COLLEGE
Tel: 01347 825 060

HOUSING CORPORATION Tel: 020 7393 2000
Website: http://www.housingcorp.gov.uk

ISPCC – IRELAND Tel: 01 679 4944
Website: http://www.ispcc.ie

LOCAL GOVERNMENT ASSOCIATION
Tel: 020 7664 3000
Website: http://www.lga.gov.uk

MEDIATION UK
Tel: 0117 904 6661
Website: http://www.mediationuk.org.uk

NATIONAL ASSOCIATION FOR THE CRIME AND RESETTLEMENT OF OFFENDERS (NACRO)
Tel: 0800 0181 259
Website: http://www.nacro.org.uk

NATIONAL NEIGHBOURHOOD WATCH ASSOCIATION
Tel: 0207772 3348
Website: http://www.neighbourhoodwatch.net
E-mail info@nnwa.org.uk

NSPCC HELPLINE
Tel: 0800 800 500
Website: http://www.nspcc.org.uk
or http://www.there4me.com

PLANNING INSPECTORATE
Tel: 0117 987 8000

RAPE CRISIS FEDERATION
Tel: 0161 272 7005

REFUGE (National Domestic Violence Helpline)
Tel: 08705 9954 4324

ROSPA – ROYAL SOCIETY FOR THE PREVENTION OF ACCIDENTS
Tel: 0121 248 2000
Website: http://www.rospa.co.uk

RSPCA Tel: 0870 55 55 999
Website: http://www.rspca.org.uk

THE SAMARITANS Tel: 08457 90 90 90
Website: http://www.samaritans.org.uk

THINK ROAD SAFETY
Website: http://www.think.dtir.gov.uk

VICTIM SUPPORT LINE Tel: 0845 30 30 900
Website: http://www.victimsupport.com

VOICE UK Tel: 01322 202 555
Website: http://www.voiceuk.clara.net
E-mail voiceuk@clara.net

WOMEN'S AID FEDERATION
Tel: 08457 023 468
Website: http://www.womensaid.org.uk

DRUGS

ADFAM
Tel: 0207 928 8900
Website: http://www.adfam.org.uk

DRUGS HELPLINE
Tel: 0800 77 66 00
Website: http://www.ndh.org.uk

DRUG MISUSE IN SCOTLAND
Tel: 0131 551 8753
Website: http://www.drugmisuse.isdscotland.org

DRUGSCOPE
Website: http://www.drugscope.org.uk

HEA DRUG CAMPAIGN (DCOS)
Tel: 01304 614 731 (England only)

HEALTH EDUCATION AUTHORITY
Tel: 0207 222 5300
Website: http://www.hea.org.uk

HEALTH EDUCATION BOARD – SCOTLAND
Tel: 0131 536 5500
Website: http://www.hebs.scot.nhs.uk

RELEASE
Tel: 0207 603 8654 (24-hour)
Website: http://www.release.org.uk

RELEASE DRUGS IN SCHOOLS ADVICE
Tel: 08457 36 66 66

RE-SOLV
Tel: 0808 800 2345 (freephone)
Website: www.re-solv.org
E-mail: Re_SolvScotland@onetel.net.uk

TACADE
Tel: 0161 745 8925
Website: http://www.tacade.com

THE SITE
Website:http://www.thesite.org.uk

TRASHED
Website: http://www.trashed.co.uk

ALCOHOL

ALANON FAMILY GROUPS UK AND EIRE AND ALATEEN
Tel: 0207 403 0888 (24-hour)
Website: http://www.al-anon.org

ALCOHOLICS ANONYMOUS Tel: 01904 644026

ALCOHOL CONCERN Tel: 0207 928 7377
Website: http://www.alcoholconcern.org.uk

ALCOHOL FOCUS – SCOTLAND Tel: 0141 572 6700

DRINKLINE Tel: 0800 917 8282 (freephone)

HEALTH PROMOTION WALES
Tel: 01222 752222
Website: http://hpw.org.uk

SCOTTISH COUNCIL ON ALCOHOL
Tel: 0141 333 9677

WRECKED
Website: http://www.wrecked.co.uk

SMOKING

ASH (Action on Smoking and Health)
Tel: 0207 224 0743
Website: http://www.ash.org.uk

ASH Northern Ireland Tel: 01232 663281

ASH Scotland Tel: 0131 225 4725

ASH Wales Tel: 01222 641101

NATIONAL CHILDREN'S BUREAU
Tel: 0207 843 6083
Website: http://www.ncb.org.uk

NETWORK VSA Tel: 01254 677493
Website: http://www.airtime.co.uk/users/sarg

QUIT (Northern Ireland) Tel: 01232 663439

QUITLINE Tel: 0800 00 22 00 (freephone)
Website: http://www.quit.org.uk

VOLATILE SUBSTANCES
Tel: 0800 77 66 00 (freephone 24-hour)

National Police Websites

Scotland

http:///www.centralscotland.police.uk
http:///www.dumfriesandgalloway.police.uk
http:///www.fife.police.uk
http:///www.grampian.police.uk
http:///www.lbp.police.uk (Lothian & Borders Police)
http:///www.northern.police.uk
http:///www.strathclyde.police.uk
http:///www.tayside.police.uk

North West

http:///www.cumbria.police.uk
http:///www.lancashire.police.uk
http:///www.merseyside.police.uk
http:///www.cheshire.police.uk
http:///www.psni.police.uk

North East

http:///www.northumbria.police.uk
http:///www.durham.police.uk
http:///www.cleveland.police.uk
http:///www.westyorkshire.police.uk
http:///www.southyorks.police.uk
http:///www.humberside.police.uk
http:///www.northyorkshire.police.uk

Midlands

http:///www.westmercia.police.uk
http:///www.staffordshire.police.uk
http:///www.west-midlands.police.uk
http:///www.leics.police.uk (Leicestershire)
http:///www.northants.police.uk (Northamptonshire)
http:///www.warwickshire.police.uk

Eastern

http:///www.derbyshire.police.uk
http:///www.nottinghamshire.police.uk
http:///www.lincs.police.uk (Lincolnshire)
http:///www.cambs.police.uk (Cambridgeshire)
http:///www.norfolk.police.uk
http:///www.suffolk.police.uk

South East

http:///www.thamesvalley.police.uk
http:///www.bedfordshire.police.uk
http:///www.herts.police.uk
http:///www.essex.police.uk
http:///www.kent.police.uk
http:///www.sussex.police.uk
http:///www.surrey.police.uk
http:///www.hampshire.police.uk

South West

http:///www.devon-cornwall.police.uk
http:///www.avonandsomerset.police.uk
http:///www.dorset.police.uk
http:///www.wiltshire.police.uk
http:///www.gloucestershire.police.uk

Wales/Cymru

http:///www.north-wales.police.uk
http:///www.dyfed-powys.police.uk
http:///www.south-wales.police.uk
http:///www.gwent.police.uk

London

http:///www.cityoflondon.police.uk
http:///www.met.police.uk

Non-Geographic Forces

http:///www.btp.police.uk (British Transport Police)
http:///www.ukaea.org.uk (UK Atomic Energy Constabulary)
http:///www.nationalcrimesquad.police.uk
Ministry of Defence Police - Tel: 01371 854000